I0114563

THE SUCCESSFUL IMMIGRANT WOMAN

8 transformational strategies to build confidence, be empowered, and achieve success as an immigrant woman

IFY A. NGWUDIKE

The Successful Immigrant Woman: 8 transformational strategies to build confidence, be empowered, and achieve success as an immigrant woman

For more information, email ingwudike@gmail.com

978-1-7774799-0-9 eBook

978-1-7774799-1-6 Paperback Book

978-1-7774799-2-3 Hardcover Book

To my family – for your love

and unfailing support.

To immigrant women – be proud of

yourselves, you have overcome a lot.

CONTENTS

GET YOUR FREE GIFT!

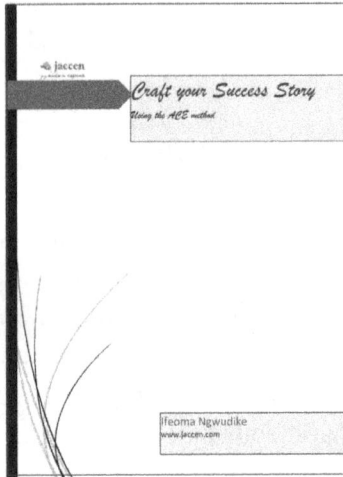

Storytelling has been used for centuries to transfer knowledge. The stories you've been telling yourself may be in the way of your success. I am glad you picked this book to work on your life journey. The Craft your Success Story workbook is a great accompaniment to this book. Download and use the workbook as you implement what you learn from this book and transform your success journey.

You can get a copy by visiting:
https://jaccen.com/resources/

INTRODUCTION

You are on a journey in life, and you will inevitably face challenges. As you set out on each new adventure, you will be excited and scared at the same time. What will the future bring? You look ahead with hope for success. But what does success mean to you? Do you know and have what it takes to be successful?

In effect, the secret to success is no secret at all. It's in you. All you need to be successful is to be aware and use the strategies in this book to get the results you need. You will know where you are headed, who you are, how to be prepared, how to learn from transitions and challenges, and how to invest in yourself while strengthening your financial stability. You will be a high-flying success!

Every woman carries a handbag most places she goes. The handbag is a part of her fashion statement in which she also carries her important personal belongings. No woman goes on a long trip without it as it contains all the tools she needs. We are told to add the skills we learn into our toolbox, but given we're women, let's grab our handbags instead of dragging along a toolbox!

In this book, I've outlined eight transformational strategies that you can always keep in your handbag. These will equip you to be successful, and you must take these strategies with you wherever you go. I've got my handbag! Hold onto yours as we go along ...

The Immigrant Experience

After living outside of my home country for over twenty years, I have discovered that the experiences immigrants face can be categorized into the following three phases:

1.   Hark-Back
2.   Hamster-Wheel
3.   Highflier

The immigrant woman who "harks-back" is nostalgic, constantly reliving what life used to be like before she left her home country. This constant comparison, with no positive outlook toward her new life, can be detrimental. In the "hamster-wheel" phase, the immigrant woman undertakes numerous actions but does not see any meaningful results. A "high-flying" experience pertains to that feeling of achieving success in many areas of life while in a new country. It is also where things seem to be flowing with more ease, and an immigrant woman aspires to be in this state every day of her journey.

I enjoy connecting and mentoring newcomers to Canada, my current country of residence, and as we share our stories, challenges, dreams, and successes, certain issues resurface repeatedly. This has led me to a deeper reflection on my own immigration journey, and I was curious to see if there were patterns or similarities in our stories. I started by asking what the differentiating factor of a successful immigrant woman could be. After several conversations with many immigrant women, I began to identify a common theme, which is summed up in the quote below.

"Extraordinary success is sequential, not simultaneous. What starts out linear becomes geometric. You do the right thing and then you do the next right thing. Over time it adds up, and the geometric potential of success is unleashed." —Gary Keller

Most people do not stumble into long-lasting success as it is a process that requires you to follow some kind of path. And in cases where luck happens, following a proven path will sustain that success.

The immigration advantage

The applications of the strategies shared in this book may differ, but the fundamental principles remain universal. Nothing I share is new. Different applications, situations, times, and seasons will influence the mix of results you may get. Still, these are the strategies many successful immigrant women—including myself—have used and continue to use in our journeys.

Applying the strategies outlined in this book equipped me with the confidence I needed to study and work on my professional certification within one year of arriving in Canada—all with the incredible support of my husband. This was after being a stay-at-home mom for ten years with four young kids: reintegrating back into the workplace and pursuing my career while maintaining a household of two adults and four children under the age of seven.

The transformational strategies that I share in this book provide relevant, actionable steps to any woman who (a) may be considering leaving her country and starting a new life in a new country, (b) is already an immigrant, recently arrived or settled-in, and (c) is going through change.

By reading this book, you will:

- Be better prepared for any journey and well equipped with key strategies in your handbag,
- Gain a deeper understanding of life and human experiences,
- Be transformed in your quest to accomplish your dream(s), and
- Become a successful and empowered woman overcoming challenges with confidence because you'll have all you need inside of you and at arm's reach in your handbag.

By applying all or some of the strategies shared in this book, you will never be stuck in the "Hark-Back" experience, and when you encounter the "Hamster-Wheel", you will know what to do to get to the "Highflyer" state in a very short time. For example, imagine that you want to cook a yummy pot of jollof rice. Knowing how to cook this dish and having the right ingredients would be of great benefit, right? Well, that's what the strategies, principles, and practical applications shared in this book will provide you on your journey.

For any woman who has already immigrated and finds herself currently in the Hark-Back or Hamster-Wheel state, this book offers you a different approach to attaining high-flying success in many areas of your life.

This is not a "how to live your life" book. Rather, it's a book on how life works from the lens of the immigration advantage. In essence, it provides you a shortcut to success on your journey!

It is divided into three parts with eight strategies to help you look at challenges from the inside out. This is because transformation always takes place from within before it manifests externally.

In this book, I will touch on principles that can be transferred from an immigration situation to any situation involving change. I hope this book speaks to everyone embarking on an adventure or embracing change in their lives. By picking up this book, you are boldly stepping into your success.

No matter your definition of success, having these strategies in your handbag is your roadmap to that success and your empowerment as an immigrant woman. So, carry that handbag with pride, sister!

PART 1

The journey begins

The dream

I hear my newly wedded husband's excited voice in my ears as he explains how beautiful my new life is going to be. Yet I am scared. As I drift away, I have flashbacks of the first time I ever left home. I see the little girl—me—being dropped off at the boarding school, and I remember the older girls running up and down the parking lot, hugging each other and chattering. They were happy, but some new students like me cried and clung to their parents, showing the emotion that others were hiding.

The memory fades as I wake up with a sigh and look around the plane. I am shocked to see two wide eyes staring curiously at me from the seat next to mine. I wonder if I muttered something aloud. The man flashes some well-arranged white teeth and asks, "So, where are you headed?"

Huh?! I almost jump out of my skin.

This is the exact question I asked myself over and over again as the days toward my departure drew ever closer. Of course, I am leaving my home country, and yes, I know the name of the country I'm moving to, given it is what my newly wedded husband calls home, but I am not sure where my life is headed. So it is startling to have a stranger sitting next to me on the plane ask me the exact question I have constantly asked myself these last few weeks. I wonder if I am that transparent?

It was my first insight into the fact that change can be scary and exciting at the same time. We all react to change differently depending on what that change may be and what caused it. So with that thought, I embraced not only my dream of a great life but also my fears, and I checked out of Nigeria (physically and mentally) as I headed for my new home in Italy.

Adventures

> *"The journey is yours. Enjoy each and every step."*
> —*Author Unknown*

How did your journey begin? I bet it started as a dream—a dream for the better, filled with excitement and pretty outcomes.

Sooner or later, the journey becomes real and starts to play out right in front of you.

Immigrating to a country is no ordinary feat. It is a transformational change. Transformational changes are always more difficult to work at. They also have a low rate of success, especially when done incorrectly. **Transformational changes are challenging. Immigration is challenging.**

Immigration is transformational because it is about a future that is largely unknown. It also incorporates a significant culture shift as it involves new ways of doing things. **Culture is our values, beliefs, assumptions, and unwritten rules. These shape our behaviors and mindset as well as our performance.** It is, therefore, no surprise that immigration has impactful consequences on immigrants, and we will take a deeper look at culture shock in part two of this book.

Mapping out your journey

Mapping out your journey and being clear about how to achieve your dream is critical to your success as an immigrant woman. There are many resources available to support you on your journey. Your strengths will provide you with the ability to think and plan, and your emotions will motivate you to succeed.

Without a plan and a map in your handbag, there is no pathway to success. And without being conscious of your emotions and reining them in, you will not have the energy and motivation for the journey ahead.

Déjà vu

"The best way to predict your future is to create it."
—Abraham Lincoln

Life in Italy had its ups and downs. Many more changes happened in my life, including motherhood and being a stay-at-home mom. These two changes triggered, once again, another dream. A dream for our children's future, a dream for better opportunities for our family, and a dream to immigrate once again!

It's 2:00 a.m., and I lie in bed tossing and turning. My family and I will leave for Canada in a couple of days. I have checked and cross-checked all the details I can think of, yet I am restless as I consider our new future. What if we run out of funds before one of us finds a paying job? How will the children adapt to change? What will their lives look like fifteen-to-twenty years from now, when they become young adults? Will they ever know our culture and language? So many thoughts ...

I remind myself that we will be fine; we must do better than we are doing now. After all, that is why my husband and I are leaving: for a better future for the children and for us. I hope there is a better future for us out there; it's the least I can hope for. I have heard of all the opportunities and the success stories. But what of the unsuccessful stories? Are there many? What are those people doing wrong? How does the dream become a nightmare? So many questions ...

I applaud the many immigrants all over the world who leave everything they have and set out in search of a dream. What courage! I now appreciate all the pains, risks, challenges, joys, and successes they have had to face. While I don't know what motivated them to make the move, I do know it all started with a dream, whether it be theirs or someone else's. So, as I toss and turn, worrying all I can—as all well-meaning mothers do—I was comforted by the fact that if we didn't pursue our dream for a better future, it would undoubtedly be one of the regrets that I would take to my grave.

I close my eyes at this thought and dream of life in Canada.

A big leap

Do you wonder where you are headed when there's a big change in your life? Immigrating to a new country is no small feat. Though people may not talk about the impact of immigration on immigrants from a life change perspective, there's no denying that it has major impacts on them as individuals, the community they've left behind, and their new community. It is a stressful life event for many.

The stress an immigrant experiences may vary at different stages of their immigrant journey. According to The TIAA Institute-GFLEC Personal Finance Index (P-Fin Index) 2020 report: "There is a seven-percentage point difference between men and women in correctly answered P-Fin Index questions. This difference is highly statistically significant. The TIAA Institute-GFLEC Personal Finance Index (P-Fin Index) measures knowledge and understanding that enable sound financial decision-making and effective management of personal finances among US adults. The P-Fin Index is an annual survey developed by the TIAA Institute and the Global Financial Literacy Excellence Center in consultation with Greenwald & Associates. It is unique in its breadth of questions and its coverage of the topics that measure financial literacy. The index is based on responses to twenty-eight questions across eight functional areas: earning, consuming, saving, investing, borrowing/managing debt, insuring, comprehending risk, and go-to information sources." There is data showing that in Canada[1] and the United States[2], immigrant women tend to face more challenges, not just compared to

---

1 https://www.criaw-icref.ca/images/userfiles/files/P4W_BN_ImmigrantWomen.pdf
2 https://statusofwomendata.org/spotlight-on-immigrant-women-poverty-opportunity-data/

immigrant men, but also compared to the women in their host country.

Considering that immigrant women make up a high percentage of immigrants, and women naturally have a big impact on the family and the children, they must know what they need to do to be successful. It is also essential that they learn how to deal with stressors that come with change and transition. These skills are a requirement of success, and such actions will inspire the generations coming after them while also positively contributing to their community.

Thankfully, many immigrant women are successful in their journey, and it is by sharing our stories and learnings that we inspire hope in others who come alongside us and those coming after us.

The dream to immigrate begins with a story, whether we are fleeing war, hunger, danger, seeking better opportunities, or reuniting with family. This dream is usually an important part of the journey, as we will see later in this chapter. I mentioned earlier how because of my marriage, I left my home country of Nigeria for Europe. And then, once kids started arriving, we moved again to seek better opportunities for our children and ourselves. My husband, whose first immigration was as a young adult, left home to seek better opportunities. He did well for himself, and when we started having a family, we had different measures of success for that season. Do we all find what we are looking for in these new places we go to? I don't know for sure. Life and its answers are not always that simple, but hopefully, the journey to find a better life leads us to fulfillment in many ways.

The dream to immigrate can have a bittersweet effect on people. Some people feel lots of excitement, right from when they decide to immigrate, and sometimes that excitement never dies. Others may have mixed feelings, sometimes feeling great and at other times wondering what they have gotten themselves into. The latter is the category I found myself in for a while. Some may dread their decision and continue to have bad experiences that feed into this fear. Whatever their feelings are, there are many reasons for these differences, but the one resounding similarity connecting all immigrants is that single decision to move from one country to another.

What was your dream? What made you leave your home country? Do you still remember that dream, and does it still hold true for you today?

There are certain things that successful immigrant women do to turn their dreams into success. Do you want to create a healthy relationship for your family, heal from past negative experiences, become a successful businesswoman, a CEO, or an amazing mom? Whatever your definition of success is, the three key concepts and strategies that you must have in your handbag as you begin to map out your journey and pursue your dreams are:

1. **Direct your journey with clarity:** Identify your why.

2. **Champion you and your journey with your identity:** Know exactly who you are and how that connects to where you are going.

Shape your path by managing transitions: Master transition planning and turn that into a powerful tool for success.

CHAPTER 1

Direct Your Journey

"You must first clearly see a thing in your mind before you can do it." —Alex Morrison

To map out your journey, you first need to be crystal clear about your destination. In other words, you need to clearly define your dream. Your journey will be full of excitement and new challenges, and a lack of clarity will kill that excitement and make the journey more challenging than it needs to be. As the person with the dream, you need to be the driver of your journey.

How does someone gain clarity about a new adventure they are about to embark on? And why is this important?

For you to direct your path, it's essential to be aware of the three different experiences immigrant women find themselves in during change, or what I call "Hark-Back", "Hamster-Wheel", and "Highflyer" phases. These three experiences are my observations of immigrant women as they go through their success paths. I briefly outlined these terms in the introduction and now provide further clarity in what follows.

I have named these experiences from words that can easily identify where you may be in your journey and help you clarify how to move along. It is important to note that these experiences are not linear, and they can happen at different points of any life change.

1. Hark-Back: This is where you hang on to what used to be. In other words, you keep going back to what was before, therefore finding it challenging to accept your new reality. This is a common feeling for most immigrants. It's not the same as homesickness, which is more of a longing. Harking back is a feeling of regret and blame for the new path that has been chosen.

An immigrant woman who continually struggles and regrets leaving her home country is not uncommon. I have also developed cold feet in many situations where I took a giant leap of faith.

It's 2:00 a.m. It is a chilly minus forty degrees Celsius, with thirty centimeters of snow outside and a howling wind. The children are running around the bedroom like they just had an overdose of sugar, and my husband is working nights at some transition job. I finally break down in a mess and ask no one in particular why I'd thought this was a good idea. We have no car, the children had not adjusted to the time difference, and it is cold.

Over the next few months, as we settled into our new home and routine, I often wondered why I'd thought moving over here with my family was a good thing to do. Nothing seemed to be exciting anymore, and this was not my definition of a blissful life. I was slowly getting bitter and unhappy with everything and everyone.

Thankfully, I did not stay in this frame of mind for much longer. However, some women never snap out of this situation. They have all sorts of challenges and struggle to find their feet. Immigrant women in this group are bitter and live in the past, forgetting why they left their home country and what they hoped to achieve. They dwell too much on the good things in the past that they cannot move forward.

According to the Cambridge Dictionary, if someone **harks back** to something in the past, they talk about it again and again, often in a way that annoys other people.

If you find yourself in this state at any point during your journey, being clear on the direction you want your journey to take will help you move on. I encourage you to refer to the clarity assessment questions at the end of this chapter for some help in gaining that clarity and focus.

2. Hamster-Wheel: Have you seen a hamster wheel? The happy hamster is moving, but he's not going anywhere. Have you ever found yourself in a similar situation? You are not just moving around in circles, but you are working pretty darn hard, too! What woman wants to be this kind of driver, working hard and going around in circles?

I've always been a hard worker, and my dad told me that a hard worker will never go hungry. Though I agree that hard work is a necessary quality for every woman, I have also seen many hardworking women who are not successful. I do not think they are doing anything wrong. They may, however, be missing some key principles that go with hard work to create success.

Hard work does not automatically equate to success. You may get the pay for your hard work but still not be successful, depending on your definition of success. This is because you may be working hard on the wrong thing. Confidence in knowing what you want and how to get it leaves you open to opportunities. This confidence gives you faith in your success journey. Just like the hamster on the wheel, an immigrant woman in this state of experience may have embraced the fact that she is now in a new place and working hard toward her dream, yet she sees no progress or success. Women in this group are in motion but not going anywhere, and unfortunately, this is where many immigrant women reside.

They may recognize that they are working very hard, even though they are not seeing the results they would have hoped to see, but they may also convince themselves that this is what it is. They become average, grinding on and repeating the words that entrap them: "This is what life abroad is like; we are working to pay our bills."

Full disclosure: I have also bought into this lie at some point, believing some common labels ascribed to immigrants, women, and people of diverse looks and culture. Other underlying conforming beliefs lend themselves to this situation, and unfortunately, many feel trapped and accept that there is no way out. But this is a lie!

There are ways out, and yes, you must work hard regardless, but believing in your dream and being clear on where you are going, coupled with hard work, will bring you successful results.

3. Highflyer: In this state, the immigrant woman is experiencing success in many areas of her life. Is this your dream? For you, what exactly does it look like to be a high-flying immigrant woman? Are you clear on that image? I am yet to meet the immigrant woman who does not want success in one or more areas of her life. I also know that many immigrant women find it uncomfortable to brag and talk about their accomplishments. So, there might be many out there who are successful but aren't comfortable sharing their story, and I am still learning how to toot my own horn, too! There is, however, a difference between acknowledging and singing your own praises and outright arrogance.

A confident woman displays self-assurance that comes from an appreciation of her attributes and talents. Frankly, this is a good way to be grateful for the gifts you have been blessed with. It also encourages other women who may be struggling or doubting themselves. Arrogance, on the other hand, is when someone makes an exaggerated show of their importance or abilities. If you have to show it, as opposed to being self-assured that you have it, that is arrogance, which is not what we are talking about here.

The high-flying immigrant woman is confident and has proven that success is attainable, despite many challenges. You will shine light on situations that others may find hopeless. This is because you have experienced success in one area of your journey. Therefore, you are more likely to experience success in others as you continue to apply the principles of success in every situation.

So, what makes the Highflyer stand out, despite the hurdles and challenges all women face? And how is all this related to the strategy of being clear and focused?

"Extraordinary success is sequential, not simultaneous."
—Gary Keller

Let me ask you a question: What made you decide to leave your country? What motivated you to embrace this challenge and take on the big adventure of uprooting yourself from home to start a new life? I pose this question to you because it is a valuable consideration to come back to whenever you arrive at a new place in your life.

What is your WHY?

Answering this question is resolved by remembering the dream that drove you to your new destination. This is important in many ways as it:

- Can serve as a strong motivator, especially when things are going sideways,
- Opens you up to see opportunities that are aligned to your reason for pursuing your dream, and

- Enables you to be crystal clear on your journey, so you do not get trapped by distractions. You will become a Highflyer, never slipping into harking back or becoming stuck on the hamster wheel because you know to bring your attention and focus back to your dream.

Imagine driving alone down an unpaved road to some deserted place you've never been to before. It's getting dark, it's raining hard, and your wipers are not working. Your windshield is covered with mud and clouded with dirt, and there's a burning smell drifting through your car as you drive. The road ahead is very unclear; you could drive into a ditch. You cannot see a way out. You may even hit obstacles on the road because you don't see them. You may also miss the turn you are supposed to take because you cannot see the signposts or traffic warnings. This can be described as a challenging situation.

I love challenges; however, in this case, I tend to easily get lost because I struggle with directions and road maps. Therefore, the scenario above would be my worst nightmare. It's very similar to the bind I found myself in as an immigrant, especially when I got to certain points where I couldn't go backward and moving forward was just as dreary. Of course, wiping my windshield is one thing that could solve a lot of my problems, and if you wear eyeglasses as I do, you'll understand the power of having clear vision.

Clear vision provides clarity, and clarity lets you see where you are going. It also lets you know how and why you need to be on that track. Because if you are not focused on what made you leave your home country to embrace your new life, you will struggle more than necessary. It will take you a lot longer to adjust and get yourself where you want to be. Also, you may never get there because you don't know why and where you want to go. Thus, the process of gaining clarity will enable you to remain focused, remember where you want to be, and empower you to get there.

How can you gain clarity?

Gaining clarity comes from having a focused path. A focused path can be determined by simply recording that path, and as a big fan of journaling, I strongly recommend that you write things down, like your needs, wants, desires, goals, requirements, etc. It's very true that when you write things down and put them in a visible place, there is a much higher chance that these goals will happen. The fact is that whether you believe it or not, it works. For example, I have written things down in the past and never looked at them again, only to find out that the exact things I desired have happened. It's magical! Journaling also helps you practice gratitude because it provides a record of things to be grateful for, especially when things are not going so well.

"After the victory, the Lord instructed Moses, "Write this down on a scroll as a permanent reminder and read it aloud to Joshua: I will erase the memory of Amalek from under heaven." —Exodus 17:14 (New Living Translation).

I encourage you to try it, and I have provided a self-assessment exercise below to help you with this reflective practice.

This assessment will help you form clarity on your dream(s) as well as where you are headed. By doing this exercise, your dream will always be vividly clear and strong in your memory so that at any step in your gigantic adventure, you can look back and say, "Yes, this is why I am doing this." You can also say with confidence, "Regardless of what may be happening—including all the detours and all the hoops to jump through—this is where I am going, and this is why I am doing it." This is a very powerful affirmation.

Self-assessment to gain clarity

If you have taken any personality self-assessments, you will usually get a report telling you about your strengths, weaknesses, and characteristics. These tools are very good at helping you find clarity.

The self-assessment questions I have here for you will not provide you with a report; however, I will guide you through a series of questions that will enable you to gain clarity and find the purpose of your dream.

Before you begin, I ask that you set aside some time to reflect so you can answer these questions as honestly as possible. Gather all the materials you need and find a comfortable place to relax with zero disturbance.

In *Hamlet*, William Shakespeare says: "To thine own self, be true." The story you tell yourself (especially at the beginning of your journey and when you face challenges) will have a big impact on your success. Remember that you are the driver, and to direct your journey and end up where you want to be, you need a road map. Clarity allows you to map out your journey. Therefore, you must be crystal clear about your vision and your dream to become a high-flying successful immigrant woman!

The 4Rs clarity self-assessment

In the 4Rs, you need to:
- Re-awaken your dream,
- Reaffirm your decision,
- Review potential challenges, and
- (W)rite your self-commitment contract.

The 4Rs are designed to be easy for you to remember whenever you encounter a situation in which you need to remain clear and focused on your plan. You can write out the 4Rs on a small card in your handbag or on a sticky note and keep that in a visible place. Therefore, when you need to be clear, re-awaken your dream, reaffirm your decision, review potential challenges, and (w)rite a self-commitment contract. I have discussed these in-depth below.

1. Re-awaken your dream:

Think back to when the desire to immigrate began. In other words, what got you here?
- What were the circumstances and the events that led to this desire?
- What is your WHY? And/or your fears?
- What was the situation, i.e., what was happening around you at the time that sparked the thought, "Hey, I need to leave; I desire to get out of here"?
- Was it just a desire, or was it an idea planted by someone else?
- Were there any subsequent events that continued to solidify this desire?

Note all these thoughts down, and you will notice that this process will re-awaken your desire and the conviction that led you to your dream.

2. Reaffirm your decision:
Reflect on how you felt and the things you did once you acknowledged that desire in the step above.

- What does success look like with this move?
- What would you need to get through and be successful?
- What research did you do? What else did you do?
- Did you check in with other people who had experienced immigration, and did you discuss with them different places to go?
- What stories did others tell you or those you told yourself that are feeding into your fears around success?

This step is important in reaffirming your why because it powers your dream and helps you focus. This is instrumental to the current state you find yourself in. Reminding yourself of these reasons and writing them down provides you with (a) a footing for the things that played into your decision to start this adventure, and (b) the groundwork to plan your next steps.

Notice that I use adventure to describe this journey because, like any adventure, it could be fun, and it could also be scary. Most adventures will get your blood pumping, and they end well with lots of learnings and growth. Similarly, these are the outcomes you will experience in this journey and will continue to experience in life generally.

In summary, this step helps you identify your reason(s) for immigrating, what it is you need to do to follow your dream, and finally, to prepare you—mentally, emotionally, physically, and spiritually—to get to that place.

Remember to write this down.

3. Review potential challenges: In this third step of establishing clarity and focus, you must think of some of the challenges you may face. By doing this, you lessen the impact of those challenges to come, and you can confidently tackle them because you anticipated them. This is because anticipating something often weakens the negative impact it may have.

When immigrating, there are common challenges that will be easily obvious. Come up with at least three and write them down. Next, brainstorm how you will deal with each of these challenges, when and if they come up at any point in your journey.

The idea here is not that you will crush all these challenges but rather will create an awareness, which will provide food to your subconscious. We often think that our conscious mind is in control when we set up plans and processes, but whether we know it or not, it is our *sub*conscious that is mostly in control. When we anticipate challenges, it helps us in the following ways:

- Thinking through this mental process prepares you to deal with these challenges. You are proactive, and as such, can mitigate some of them before they occur.
- It heightens your awareness and increases your openness to opportunities that may present themselves when these challenges come your way. It could be as simple as noticing when someone is going through something similar and seeing how they deal with it. Or it could be acting proactively to ensure that you do not have to meet those challenges. As mentioned earlier, your subconscious will

often take over if you have prepared and planned for such scenarios.

In summary, this step helps you to formulate solutions to potential challenges so they can be pulled out if you need them.

4. (w)Rite your self-commitment contract: Finally, after you have established your conviction as to why, where, and what will help you to be successful, you should now have a plan to meet any challenges that may show up. The next step is to sit down and make a contract with yourself. Yes—a contract with yourself.

You're probably asking, why make a contract with yourself? And what will this achieve in helping you with clarity? Well, a contract helps you remain firm in your decision, it keeps you accountable, and it recognizes that though there might be detours, you are committed to the process. There will be hoops to jump and mountains to climb, but your eyes will be set on that north star where you are headed. Furthermore, your contract does not mean you are inflexible; rather, it serves you when there is a detour as well as when the path is planned because you know with conviction and certainty where you are going.

The contract will illustrate milestones—some of which you will have accomplished, depending on the stage of your journey to success. Making this contract will, therefore, always give you a reason to celebrate your journey!

Action:

- Get yourself a journal or a notebook.
- Complete the assessment above.

- Summarize your why in one sentence and put this in a visible place such as in your handbag, or on a sticky note on your mirror, or in your phone— wherever you will see it often.

Recap

The immigration adventure is a complex yet transformational journey. To be a successful immigrant woman, you must direct your journey because no one else knows your dream as well as you do. Gain clarity and focus to be aware of the experiences you may find yourself in, so you know what to do to be successful.

- As an immigrant woman, you will go through these experiences in your immigrant journey:
  ◇ Harking back
  ◇ Running on a hamster wheel
  ◇ Being a highflyer
- For you to achieve your dream, you need to have clarity and focus. By using the 4Rs of the clarity self-assessment provided in this chapter, you will be equipped with a tool to map out your journey.

By re-assessing your dream, reaffirming your decision, reviewing what challenges lie ahead, and writing your self- commitment contract, you empower yourself to tackle your dream and confidently succeed in all that you do.

Fun fact: I wear eyeglasses, and I always keep an extra pair in my handbag. For me, this symbolizes clarity of vision along with my 4 Rs. What's in your handbag that prompts you to focus?

In the next chapter, we will explore what role "identity" plays in change management.

CHAPTER 2

Be Your Own Champion

"When I discover who I am, I'll be free." —Ralph Ellison

In chapter one, we discussed clarity of vision and how focusing on your dream directs your path. However, this is not enough to be successful in your adventure. There are times when you will lose yourself and get sidetracked as you travel the road of life as an immigrant. Knowing yourself is an essential aspect of every stage of your life's adventure.

Where did I go?

"How are you?" my mom asked.
"We're fine!" I responded.
"That's wonderful, dear, but how are you doing?"
Mom repeated.

Hmmm! Maybe she didn't get my initial response? Sometimes long-distance calls are not so clear ...

"We are doing well, Mom!" I said, this time a bit louder so she could hear better.

"Yes, but I mean, how are YOU?" she said again.

Okay, now I was getting a bit concerned. What could be wrong with Mom? She wasn't making sense, repeating the same question over and over. "Are you okay?" I inquired softly with concern in my voice.

All I heard was a soft chuckle. Then my mom told me not to change the subject, because she was concerned about me. About me?! This was an interesting conversation, and maybe Dad could help me out here. So I ask for Dad, but Mom said she needed me first to tell her how I was doing.

She went on to explain that for the past six years, anytime she asked how I was doing, I didn't respond to that specific question. While I was still trying to recover from this confusing interaction, pointing out that I always told her how we were doing, she stopped me mid-sentence.

"How many are YOU?" she asked. "This is my concern; each time I ask how YOU are doing, all I get is WE are doing well. So, tell me, how are YOU?"

Oh my! It all suddenly dawned on me. She wanted to know how I (just I) was doing. Then the truth hit me—I actually didn't know! I had long since stopped thinking about myself and how I was doing. With one preschooler, two toddlers, and a baby, I had completely lost myself. And I didn't even know it until my mom spelled it out for me!

So, I asked myself, Who am I? Who have I become? And who am I becoming? I was functioning, making sure everyone was fine, but I was not caring much about me, my appearance, my personal growth—nothing! The rest of the family was my priority. And I guessed that if everyone else was fine, then I must also be fine.

Consider how many women have lost themselves once, twice, or many times in their life journey. How about you? Have you lost or buried your identity? Are you waiting for the years when you can get yourself back to those good old days? I was very grateful to my mom for bringing that fact to my awareness.

Self-awareness and identity

"So, I guess we are who we are for a lot of reasons. And maybe we'll never know most of them. But even if we don't have the power to choose where we come from, we can still choose where we go from there. We can still do things. And we can try to feel okay about them."
—Steven Chbosky

Your identity and self-awareness go together. As an immigrant woman, you may struggle with identity in many ways. Your identity includes your culture, your race/ethnicity, whether you are single or married, if you have children or not, if you are a career mom or stay-at-home mom ... And the list goes on.

Immigration can be an arduous journey, and it's not a journey that anyone starts without a valid reason.

Many challenges will rear their head during the first few years of your adventure (more on that in the coming chapters). These challenges include a lack of friends, family, or support network, finding a job, navigating new sets of norms/culture, and so many others. However, the good news is you can get through these challenges more easily because of what you will learn in this book.

Earlier in my husband's immigration journey, he did menial jobs to make ends meet. He recalls his struggles with the language barrier—for example, how he would smile when he was being disrespected because he didn't know what was being said. He remembers being so scared once. He had run out of money and didn't know where his next meal would come from. He did not know what he would say to his family back home, who were looking forward to the money he would send them.

Yet, in Nigeria, as the owner of a thriving business, he would never have found himself in these situations. It was harsh to accept, but his search for peace and opportunities helped him focus during those periods of hardship.

The point here is that challenges we face can easily make our dream more of a nightmare at times. Many immigrants are thriving in their new countries. With resilience, many immigrants forge ahead, become successful, and go on to empower others. It is my hope that you will be one of these successful dreamers who realizes her dreams.

Like me, many women are aware they will face some challenges. They prepare themselves to brace for whatever may come their way. Truthfully, nothing fully prepares us for some of the challenges we meet. However, when interacting and speaking with other immigrant women from different backgrounds, one thing stands out as a key ingredient to success. **Know yourself!**

There's no denying that, at times, you may struggle with who you are. After my strange phone conversation with my mom, I realized I had lost my identity when I started having children. This, of course, was not intentional. It crept up on me, and I remained oblivious until she called it out.

This loss of identity is common with changes and transitions in life, and if you are not aware of it, you will struggle without knowing what the problem is. Self-identity is very powerful for women because it can act as an anchor in times of stress. Self-identity is defined by the Oxford Dictionary as *"the recognition of one's potential and qualities as an individual, especially in relation to social context."*

Do you have a strong sense of your identity? The topic of identity for many immigrant women takes numerous shapes that can be muddied by culture, religion, education, motherhood, life seasons/age, and social standing. As immigrant women begin to emerge and reshape their identity, some blossom and burst from many positive outcomes while others languish in family struggles and misunderstandings. This has negative impacts on their mental health and overall wellness.

I couldn't agree more with Ralph Ellison, who said in his book, *The Invisible Man*, that "One is free when they discover who they are."

A woman who knows herself is a gift to the world. She's confident and powerful. She influences people, communities, and the circles she moves in because she is not swayed or defined by what is happening around her. She is focused, gets results, and is successful.

As an immigrant woman, knowing your identity and your purpose becomes an anchor because things will be thrown at you from all angles, things will be said that may hurt you or lift you up, life may feel unjust and unfair at times, you may feel lonely and alone, and you will have a gazillion questions and moments of insecurity and uncertainty. You may also experience harking-back and hamster-wheeling at various moments. Yet, in all of this, you will rise up and stand tall because, more than anyone else, you know who you are and where you are headed.

How can you regain your identity?

"Never forget what you are, for surely the world will not. Make it your strength. Then it can never be your weakness. Armor yourself in it, and it will never be used to hurt you." —George RR Martin

The issue of identity loss can be so subtle that a woman may not even recognize she's lost herself, or when the process started, and how far she has gotten toward losing herself.

After the "aha" moment during that phone conversation with my mom, I didn't flip the switch right away. I recognized that it had taken a few years to lose myself, so regaining myself in my new reality would be a journey of its own. The good thing was that I knew I was lost and needed to find "me" again.

One Sunday afternoon after mass, my family and I had stopped by the mall to pick up some craft items for my son's project, and as we passed by a big retail store, a friendly lady asked me if I would like to have a free makeup consultation. Well, as you can imagine, at that time I didn't use makeup or think much about myself at all. I smiled and politely declined the offer, but my husband (poor guy, having to put up with me in shapeless sweat suits and pulled-up bun hair all those years), in his infinite wisdom, nudged me gently to give it a try. He shrugged as he pointed out that we were not in a hurry. "Besides," he said, "the lady is quite friendly."

So, I sat down with no interest in this whole business and let the lady do her thing. A few minutes later, she called my husband and kids to come over and whirled me around. First, their mouths dropped open in shock, then the flashing teeth were followed by my youngest son asking what I guess everyone else was thinking. "Is that my mommy? She's so pretty," he said with a wide grin. All of this happened so quickly that I was confused, then embarrassed, and asked for the mirror.

I gasped when I saw my reflection! I couldn't even recognize myself! Wow! "What have you done to me?" I asked the lady at the store. I was literally transformed!

She was intrigued to learn from my family that they'd never seen me in any makeup. Then she reassured me that I was not alone in this struggle. She had seen this happen to a lot of women who became lost once they'd experienced a significant life change. Then she made this interesting comment that has stuck with me since then. "Don't worry, you can always find yourself again in little ways—just like we did with this makeup."

I thanked her for the excellent job and bought some of the makeup, even though I was certain there was no way I could recreate whatever she had just done to my face. However, this encounter was an enlightening moment in my journey of self-discovery.

Here's what I discovered as I reflected on this experience:

- There are lots of women who do not know themselves and live through the lens of other people around them.
- For a woman, losing herself happens at different stages of life. For example:
  ◇ During the teenage/adolescent years,
  ◇ As young adults,

◊ When there's a change in social and marital status,

◊ During motherhood,

◊ In times of loss,

◊ As a result of immigration, etc.

• Loss of self-identity is seasonal. Some women may not be aware that they no longer know themselves. The women who recognize this fact and are aware that it's a seasonal change are the empowered women in our midst and who we strive to become.

• And the most important lesson I learned was that it only takes a little act to find yourself again, and once you find yourself, you will discover freedom.

That day, after seeing the joy on the faces of my husband and children, I realized I was not helping them by defining myself through them. I was more than my children's mom or my husband's wife. I may have prioritized their needs over mine; however, the truth is that no one can give what they do not have. Right there, in that store, I resolved that from then on, I would rediscover myself because no one else could do that for me. I am unique! I am fearfully and wonderfully made, and I cannot give my family (or the world) what I am meant to give them if I do not know who I am or what my life's purpose is.

What next?

Once you become aware that you have lost yourself, you should start the journey of redefining and rediscovering who you are and who you want to be. Self-awareness is the ability to see yourself clearly and objectively through reflection and introspection. Though this practice is individual, in my case, I found I needed help to be able to reflect objectively. Working with a life coach helped me save the many years I had lost and fast-tracked my journey to success. Getting help when you need it is okay, and I encourage you to explore the support of a coach or other professional for different areas of your life.

My research in writing this book included many interviews with immigrant women from various parts of the world. Identity stood out as a common and big concern (and to mothers, it was a concern for their children as well). It was also identified as a key source of empowerment, equipping women for many life accomplishments.

They expressed that identity gave them freedom—freedom because they aligned their decisions, which therefore provided them with reactions and priorities in line with their values and identity. They were more comfortable in their own skins, irrespective of what was happening around them. This does not make them superwomen who don't feel pain; rather, they were assured that no matter what, they knew the truth about themselves, who they were, and what their purpose in life was. They were anchored to this truth, and that is very powerful.

Proven benefits of self-awareness

"I praise you because I am fearfully and wonderfully made; your works are wonderful; I know that full well."
—Psalm 139:14 (New International Version)

Now, let's shift our attention to the benefits of being self-aware.

As you've gathered by now, there are many benefits to being self-aware and knowing yourself aside from being free. Imagine if you found yourself experiencing harking-back or hamster-wheeling. Exploring who you are and who you want to be will jolt you into action because now you know better, and you won't want to stop yourself from becoming that high-flying woman. Exciting, right?!

> *"Do the best you can until you know better. Then when you know better, do better." —Maya Angelou*

And if you are not convinced, here are some other benefits of being self-aware:

- **Proactiveness:** Because you know yourself, self-awareness helps you to be proactive. You know what you want; therefore, you can anticipate opportunities and/or challenges. This helps you plan accordingly and line up the resources and support you need to manage change and adjust. Being proactive leads to better decision-making, openness to opportunities, and the ability to bounce back when things go wrong.

- **Acceptance:** Self-awareness boosts your acceptance of yourself and encourages the acceptance of others. It allows you to see things from their perspective, which is a skill you will need if you are to quickly integrate into a new environment.

- **Self-control:** A self-aware immigrant woman practices self-control. This is very much needed when your buttons are being pushed. As an immigrant woman, you may have experienced or witnessed some horrid things or heard firsthand stories of what other women have gone through. All these experiences will be stored in your memory bank, and there's no telling where and when your buttons will be pushed. Being self-aware can help you manage sensitive situations and empower you to react appropriately.

• **Confidence:** Lastly, being self-aware results in being confident and proud of oneself. Not only will you know with confidence what you want and what you are capable of, but you will also be a role model for other women, your family, and the entire community. Imagine the legacy you could build as a confident immigrant woman!

The list above is by no means exhaustive, but it is my hope that it encourages you to find your identity. Self-awareness has the potential to enhance every experience you have. It's a practice that can be used at any time to ground yourself in the moment. In my case, being self-aware has helped me overcome many barriers in my career and personal life as I am confident in dealing with unknowns, learning new things, speaking up when I need to advocate for myself, and teaching my children and other women to do so, too. We are all fearfully and wonderfully made, and that knowledge is powerful in accepting our uniqueness.

Self-awareness questions to help you discover your identity

For you to connect with your unique identity, be comfortable with who you are, and know your values, it is important to develop a good sense of self-awareness. The following questions provide guidance on this journey of self-exploration and self-discovery to define (or, in my example above, redefine) who you are.

First, pull out your journal and record your reflections. The act of writing is powerful, especially when you go back to these reflections later. You will be surprised at how much you have accomplished and written down. This is because, as I mentioned in the previous chapter, **success is sequential.**

Answer these questions:
- How would you describe yourself using three words?
- What dreams and goals do you have?
- What is currently keeping you from achieving these dreams and goals?
- Name the three to five most important things in your life.
- How much time are you giving to them?
- How satisfied are you in your current relationship with those important things you identified above?
- What is your biggest strength?
- What is your biggest weakness?
- How would you describe the ideal YOU?
- If you left the world today, what one thing will people say about you? What legacy would you leave behind?

Action:

- Open your journal or notebook.
- Complete the assessment above.

- Write an affirmation on something you have discovered about yourself during this exercise. Repeat
this affirmation at least once a day. For example,
here's an affirmation I repeat to myself every morning: "Lord, I am open to your amazing possibilities."
This helps me start the day with an expectation
of all the good things that will happen to me and
through me.

Recap

An immigrant woman's journey is marked with lots of transitions, and at some point, you may lose yourself. If you don't
invest time in redefining who you are, you may lose your
clarity, and your confidence will be negatively impacted. To
unwrap your unique gift as an immigrant woman, you must
regain your lost identity (if lost) or, if you know yourself well,
keep working from a place of self-awareness.

Identity and self-awareness are vital to you as an empowered immigrant woman. You are confident and know yourself
better than anyone else.

Due to the many cycles, seasons, and life changes a woman
goes through, you may lose your identity. You may have lost
yourself once or many times, and you may not even be aware
of it. Do not worry. You can regain your identity by engaging in
simple, caring, and enjoyable acts that boost your self-esteem.
They help you rediscover your beauty and can be simple, like
using makeup again, or any other form of self-care.

Getting to know yourself is a very powerful and worthwhile endeavor. And as a self-aware immigrant woman, you
are a high-flying success in many areas of your life. You are

powerful and exude confidence, thereby being a strong role model to other women. The self-awareness questions above will help you get to know yourself and fast-track your success.

And finally, your daily affirmation, which encapsulates your identity, is a must-have item for your handbag.

Fun fact: The following items in my handbag are symbols of my identity—my compact handbag mirror and my photo ID. Is there any item you have that reminds you of who you are or who you want to become?

In chapter three, we focus on how change and transitions are driving forces. Mastering transitions will help you manage change effortlessly while also driving the transformation that's bound to happen on your journey.

CHAPTER 3

Shape your Path

"But today our very survival depends on our ability to stay awake, to adjust to new ideas, to remain vigilant and to face the challenges of change." —Martin Luther King Jr.

In the first chapter, we established why you are where you currently find yourself. You also worked on being clear and focused on the journey ahead of you because you are internally motivated by your "why"—the reason why you embarked on this journey to uproot your life and start all over again.

Armed with that clarity of vision, in chapter two, you reflected on who you are. By knowing yourself and your values, you can develop strategies to manage any storms that may happen on your journey. Your self-awareness and identity provide an anchor—that grounding factor that sustains and upholds you during the twists and turns of your journey.

In chapter three, we discuss the last of the three foundational strategies on your path to success. You do not want just to hold on to your dream; you want to bring it to life. And knowing this is not going to be an easy journey is not enough to lead you down that road. You also need the skills to navigate your path with more ease and less pain. The transition process can be seen as the bridge connecting where you are to your dream and your destination.

The life map

I believe very strongly that when women are empowered, they, in turn, empower generations. My grandma, who lived to be over 120 years old, was a powerful woman. Her dad, who was made a warrant chief[3] when the British came to our village, believed that girls should be empowered. In those days, this was very different and bold thinking.

Grandma did not have any formal education, but she was brought up to have a voice and use it. She had twelve children but lost many of them, and her husband, while she was still young. Being smart and understanding the power of women, she organized other widows to start a co-op and buy back their husbands' lands, which had been taken from them.

Grandma had already bought back all her husband's landed property and more. Back in those days, power and wealth were based on landed property as owners could lease out their farmlands. (Actually, today, this is not much different, as a successful immigrant woman builds wealth by increasing her net worth.) She then decided to make sure other women could do the same.

---

3 https://www.encyclopedia.com/history/encyclopedias-almanacs-transcripts-and-maps/warrant-chiefs-africa

I still hear my grandma saying education gives one a place at the table. She made sure her children, grandchildren, great and great-great-grandchildren went to school. She taught me to find and use my voice as an Igbo woman because a woman is a powerful gift to every community. Since my primary school days, I have been told by teachers, family, friends, and colleagues that I have a quiet yet powerful voice, both literally and figuratively.

I'm ready to join forces with other women to serve and empower an army of women by helping them with their success journeys—whatever their definitions of success are.

This story has been an inspiration to me, and I was able to put it into words after I completed a life map exercise. It gives me the confidence to pursue my dreams and inspire other women. There are so many stories in history that portray the courage, bravery, and powerful impact women have had directly and indirectly in our communities.

What's your story?

At the young age of eleven, I left the safety of my home, parents, and siblings to join hundreds of other young girls in our pre-teen and teenage years at a boarding school very far away from home. I lived with other kids and teenagers with little adult supervision, and it would be my new home for ten months of every year for the next six years. This was the first major change in my life that I can remember. There was a lot of structurein boarding school, and as a child, I did not think about that life as a transition. For the first two years, I remember being homesick for many weeks when I went back to school after the holidays. In hindsight, I realize this was my introduction to change.

It was as a young adult in my early twenties that I was forced to start thinking about change and transition. This was quite different from the independence I'd had when I left home for secondary school, and university.

Marriage was another big life change—life was no longer about only me. My identity changed as I took on a new last name, and I also went through other changes as a result of getting married. Changes such as leaving my home country to live with my husband, who was living and working on another continent. This was scary, of course—getting married and moving so far away to live where I knew only one person. Reflecting on my first immigration experience, I recognize how it prepared me for our next move. Though I had this experience under my belt, I will also be the first to admit that the next move was very different from the first.

I share a little bit of my life map because the way of my people is to tell stories. Stories have always been the way we convey not only our history but also our values. And why is this important? There is power in stories. They impact us in ways we may not be conscious of. As you start a new life, it is beneficial to explore what your story is up to the present moment.

A life map exercise can help you identify the stories that have shaped your life so far and those which may continue to shape your future. Knowing these stories will help you tell your own story, or conversely, rewrite your story as you move ahead. Your story will be unique to you and should inspire you and others—that is how powerful mine about my grandma and her inspiration is to me.

Your "life map" is a tool you can use to explore the different factors that have shaped who and where you are today. These factors influence how you feel, how you relate to others, and how you interpret and experience the way others relate to you. Through the process of doing a life map exercise, you will gather your life data and use this information to focus on the areas of your life that will lead you to growth, success, and freedom.

What is a life map?

A life map tracks your journey through life and marks out **important events** along the way.

In the previous chapter, we talked about transformational change being challenging because:

1. It involves the future,
1. It involves new ways of doing things, and
1. It involves a significant culture change.

A life map will help you during a time of transition as it shows you the journey you have been on to that point and how you can use it to shape your future.

The Life Map Exercise

As every person is a unique individual with a unique story, the life map exercise is also individual. Some people will finish it quickly, and others will take longer. To do this exercise, I would recommend you set aside some time for it, especially if you have not done this type of exercise before.

The process may awaken many pleasant experiences, but as a warning, it may also awaken uncomfortable past experiences as well. If an unpleasant experience is triggered, it may be an opportunity for healing. Remember that these stories, whether we know it or not, have had a powerful impact in shaping our paths.

Ready?

To begin your life map, gather some supplies such as paper, writing and drawing materials, or digital tools such as slides, word-processing tools like MS Word or Google Docs, spreadsheets, apps, etc., and set aside a few hours to reflect as you answer the questions below.

Before you begin, remind yourself why you are doing this exercise. The stories you tell yourself shape your life. This exercise will help you identify the patterns of your story and the impact these have on the things you do in life. They will also highlight what parts of your story can help you shape the path you are on now.

1. Where did you start your life journey? Travel back in your memories to when you were a baby.
2. Where have you been in your life? This could include places or events.
3. Where are you now? You can think of this geographically, seasonally, your age, etc.
4. Where would you like to go? What are your plans for the future, financially, health-wise, location, etc.?
5. How will you get there? Transition planning acts as a bridge between where you currently are and where you would like to be.
6. What will affect whether you'll get there? This is similar to the exercise above, where you discovered

yourself and explored what challenges you might encounter.

What kind of events will you include in your life map?

To answer the questions above, you must look at important life events during different stages of your life journey. These will guide you as you trace your story. The focus here is on those life events that were transformational, not just incremental. These could include:

- Events that taught you about life, e.g., moving to boarding school taught me to advocate for myself.
- Events that inspired and motivated you, e.g., the story about *ogu umu nwanyi, or the Aba Women's riot* [4] in Eastern Nigeria in 1929, taught me how women can use their voices to impact societal change.
- Events that made you feel grown up, e.g., as the first child of my parents, I remember feeling a lot of responsibility for my younger siblings and as a young child being the leader in many ways.
- Events that highlight the gifts you have received in life and teach us more about appreciating them when they are there, e.g., the loss of a loved one.

You will notice as you recall and reflect on these important life events that, regardless of whether you see these events as good or bad, they help you appreciate your life, adapt to your unique circumstances, and shape your future.

---

4 https://www.encyclopedia.com/history/encyclopedias-almanacs-transcripts-and-maps/igbo-womens-war

What does your life map look like?

Like any map, your life map can be made up of photos, texts, arrows, symbols, labels, and numbers—whatever symbolizes those important events and how they connect to your present story. While doing this exercise, you may notice certain patterns in your life, gain better clarity about why you are on your current journey, and start to focus more sharply on where you are going and how to get there.

The old new ways

"Light precedes every transition. Whether at the end of a tunnel, through a crack in the door, or the flash of an idea, it is always there, heralding a new beginning."
—Teresa Tsalaky, author of The Transition Witness.

I'm always excited when I get a new mobile phone. Well, until I spend twenty minutes trying to find my favorite app. Then frustration kicks in. I start to remember how easy things were with my old phone. I now have to access apps differently, the home screen is strange, and there are lots of things I must set up before I can use it easily. Does this sound familiar? Have you noticed how you go back to old ways even when you are in a new phase? My mobile phone experience is just one of many tiny transitions and changes we often go through.

Every transition begins with an ending. The first time I read that, I thought to myself, "What are we talking about here?" In my mind, transitioning is all about the new journey. And I am not alone in this thinking. Many of us dive right into a new beginning without ending the old one. But we must let go of some things before we can pick up the new ones—not just outwardly but inwardly as well.

Change and transition are very important in life because, without these, we cannot grow. It is by leaving our comfort zones that we grow exponentially, and that is what immigration is for all immigrant women. Not one of us remains the same. I recently read a book called *Transitions: Making Sense of Life's Changes*[5] by William Bridges. He gave the following apt clarification on the difference between change and transition—two words often used interchangeably.

According to Bridges, **change** refers to a specific event such as a new job, becoming a parent, losing a loved one, etc. However, **transition** is not nearly as linear or concrete. Instead, **transition** is the process we go through in response to change.

> *"Transition is psychological; Change is situational. It is not events, but rather the inner reorientation and self-redefinition that you have to go through in order to incorporate any of those changes into your life."*
> —William Bridges

In my understanding, transition involves not only your hopes and fears but also a transformational process. It is internal because you must come to terms with the new situation, while change involves external events. For a few reasons, from an immigrant woman's perspective, this distinction between change and transition is important:

- Change is constant in life, and since transition is a response to change, it's vital to the success or failure of any change process and its outcomes.

5 Bridges Transition Model.

"Success or failure during the transition period is a strong predictor of overall success or failure in the job." (Prof. Michael Watkins, January 2009, Picking the Right Transition Strategy, Harvard Business Review)[6] Knowing that you have a framework to manage change is a step in the right direction toward success. Implementing the framework for transition planning, which involves an inner psychological process, puts you ahead of the game with any change you experience.

• I once had a boss at work who was a great leader. When he left the organization, I struggled with the idea that I had a new boss and things were different. In recognizing that this event was not going to be the last time I would experience such a change, I was motivated to approach that change differently. In other words, it was that internal resolve that led me to further research the personal transition process. I am now equipped to handle similar changes with better success.

• When change happens—planned or unplanned—we tend to adjust or resist it, regardless of success. I don't know about you, but my first reaction to change is often resistance—including mental resistance. It's almost always my knee-jerk reaction to change, even if it's just momentary. Then, my next reaction is to adjust, accept, and embrace, or simply grab the change and run with it.

• For any of these responses to happen, some internal work must go on. Sometimes, it may seem like the acceptance was swift, but when you find

---

6 https://hbr.org/2009/01/picking-the-right-transition-strategy

yourself revisiting old ways, it means the transition is not complete. Resisting change is a futile endeavor. Telling someone who is resisting change that they will someday succumb to it is almost like pouring water on a rock. This is because when you resist change, it causes a lot of stress, fear, and anxiety. These reactions reduce your ability not only to function properly but also to process information. This is not a good place to be if success is your goal because when under stress, people tend to react to perceived threats rather than to reality. Therefore, this can derail you from your journey, and you will end up missing opportunities.

• Without internalizing the transition process through unlearning and letting go of our previous ways, when change happens, success eludes us. We may adapt to change with coping mechanisms and/or employing external systems that may have worked well for someone else; however, until we go through the transition process, we may keep seeking something that we cannot name.

"No one sews a piece of unshrunk cloth on an old garment. If he does, the patch tears away from it, the new from the old, and a worse tear is made. And no one puts new wine into old wineskins. If he does, the wine will burst the skins—and the wine is destroyed, and so are the skins. But new wine is for fresh wineskins."
—Mark 2:21-22 (English Standard Version)

This internal work involves:

◇ Unlearning whatever worked for you in previous situations. You will need to learn new ways to adapt to change and master them. This is hard work, and therefore it is not surprising that we tend to resist change. But as an immigrant woman, it's impractical to continue responding this way because some of the ways you approached things previously may no longer work in a new place. And not engaging in the unlearning process impedes your success, much like harking back. *"People with hammers will treat everything like a nail, even when the job at hand may be better accomplished with a drill or a saw."* —Mark Twain.

◇ Letting go of the old ways and accepting new beginnings. This is easier said than done. It can be done, and nature provides us with examples of endings and beginnings. Think of the seasons. They don't start abruptly. Rather, there is a gradual end and a marked beginning. Life is available for all living things: humans, animals, plants, etc., and there seems to be a seamless transition in the order of nature where transformation happens (i.e., a butterfly, which originates from a caterpillar). There's no room for resistance. An embryo turns into a human, and seeds become plants. We could certainly borrow a leaf from nature in how we approach our own transitions.

◇ Recognizing that to achieve success, you need courage, grit, perseverance, and humility. You can be confident that putting in the effort and work will not be wasted but instead will yield fruit that will multiply. *"That person is like a tree planted by streams of water, which yields its fruit in season and whose leaf does not wither—whatever they do prospers."* —Psalm 1:3 (New International Version)

Transition planning: Shape your path

Transition planning involves planning for a new environment. One of my favorite analogies about shaping my path can be compared to my position on a bus. I have provided two examples under scenario 1 and scenario 2 below.

Scenario 1:

I take the public bus to work, and I usually get on at the bus terminal. My journey is about forty minutes long, and there are more than twenty stops before mine. So, many people get on and off this bus during my forty-minute ride. I also have no control over any part of this journey aside from when I request to get on or off the bus.

Scenario 2:

In another example, I take the bus to a city far from my home. I have never been there before, so I am completely at the mercy of the bus driver. I have an address but no clue how to get there, what direction I should go in, or where I should get off. I just hope the driver will tell me when we get there.

Can you see how very <u>not</u> empowering scenario 2 is?

Scenario 2 is how the life of an immigrant starts—at least for most. To feel more confident and less anxious about this kind of trip, it is important to ask yourself, "What could I do?" Understanding your options will support your journey. This is why clarity of purpose is important. So, let's consider our options as the driver or the passenger.

1. The driver makes the decisions on the routes to take, what detours to make, where to stop, how to handle speed bumps, and when to slow down or speed up. If you did some homework as a passenger, you could have some influence over the driver by requesting they stop for you at a certain location. But ultimately, the driver is in control. Think here for a moment. Are you behind the steering wheel, making the decisions?

    Yes, I recognize being the driver may not be possible or even practical. You may also choose to use other modes of public transport, carpool, or use your own personal vehicle or rental, etc. But even in these cases, you have some influence by pre-planning or researching options such as choice of vehicle. You could also have acquired a map and followed the route you were being taken on so you would know when a wrong or unnecessary turn was being made. You could have prepared yourself by knowing points of interest and restaurants along the way, enabling you to stop for a break and a stretch.

    The point is to figure out how you want your experience to be. You may need to be a driver at certain times and at other times a passenger. Be prepared and work out how you would play those roles and shape your journey.

2. As a passenger, you have minimal control over the trip. This isn't good or bad; it totally depends on what you want from your journey. It also includes other factors like who you are with, your level of competence, etc. As a passenger, things are more up to chance, luck, fate, or wherever the wind blows.

My family often goes on road trips, and we enjoy it. However, I do not enjoy driving, even within the city. I mostly drive out of necessity, so I can happily be a passenger most of the time. When my husband or son are the drivers, I can sleep throughout the trip because we are on the same page. They know the plan and are with me. Things are different when I don't really know the driver. I feel unsafe and stressed. At times like this, I'd rather be driving. In other words, my safety and control over the situation trump my dislike for driving. Therefore, I totally get it if you also love being a passenger most of the time.

A word of caution, though. Because a passenger does not have control, they cannot direct the path they travel upon. Therefore, to shape your path (and be in charge of your story or your own life journey), you have to be the driver. Always. No one else can do this for you. You can get help, of course, but ultimately, you have to take charge to get where you want to be.

While you can't control everything that happens on your life trip (i.e., detours, road construction, or unexpected dead ends), you can do some pre-planning to help you along the way.

Shaping your path pre-planning guide

"Failing to plan is planning to fail." —Benjamin Franklin

Sticking to the driving analogy from above and finding ways of getting and staying "behind the wheel", ask the following questions as you plan:

- Do you know where you want to go and why? For assistance, refer to your answers to the clarity questions from chapter 1.

- Are you relying on someone else—or some idea that may not be meaningful to you—for your life and journey? Why is that? Use your answers to the self-awareness questions in chapter 2 to help you work out your self-identity.

- Are there any "road construction obstacles" ahead? What challenges are you aware of or should you plan for? How would you handle them when and if they come up? The tools in the self-awareness section will also help you answer these questions.

- And lastly, is your "car" ready for what might be a lengthy trip? Life is a journey, and you want to enjoy most of it. In the Bible, we are told in John 10:10 (Christain Standard Bible): "I have come so that they may have life and have it in abundance." To enjoy this awesome promise, you must be prepared for the time, energy, and resources you will expend. Giving and getting is the natural order of things, so be prepared to live life fully and in abundance by giving life fully and in abundance.

With these preparation tips, you will have an enjoyable trip, so sit back and celebrate.

The 3 stages of the Bridges Transition Model

Change can be scary! Handling change well will make things better, life easier, and fast-track your journey to success. The Bridges Transition Model is one of the tools that help guide you through transitions.

As an organizational consultant, William Bridges found that guiding people through transition was the key to successful change. He identified three stages of transition, and his model strives to help business leaders to understand the feelings people experience as they are guided through a change process.

The three stages of the Bridges Transition Model and its application for an immigrant woman

Earlier, we looked at the difference between change and transition. We identified change as an external event that happens in your life, while transition involves the internal process you go through when change happens. The transition process is different for everyone. You are unique, and therefore your journey is unique to you. Recognize that this is your story and know that your path to change will be different from those of other people. This system will support you through changes that are a constant in everyone's lives. The three stages of transition that Bridges identified are:

1. Ending,
2. The neutral zone, and
3. The new beginning.

We'll discuss each of these stages in turn.

Stage 1: Ending and letting go

I was looking for what to wear to the office end-of-year party and I saw the pretty red dress I've had since before I had my first child. I took it out, admired it, and with a big sigh, hung it back in the closet. I couldn't let it go, even though I knew I would never fit into that dress again. Why couldn't I let it go? Logically, I knew I was done with this dress, but emotionally, I was still tied to it. The dress reminded me of how I was more than twenty years ago, and in some sense, part of me wanted to look like that or, should I say, be able to fit into that size again.

Chances are you have a similar story, maybe not with a dress but with something or someone else. It's normal to experience an emotional reaction if something you like is being replaced. Acknowledging the end of an era and the beginning of another helps you let go. In some way, by holding on to this red dress for many years, I was denying the fact that I needed to do some work on my health and wellness, which at the time, was my current reality. In letting go, I began to recognize that by not doing the work I needed to do on my health, I was holding back from achieving my future goals.

How are you feeling? This stage will feel like an "emotional wilderness zone". Acknowledging the emotions you are feeling and giving yourself the patience to work things out internally is a healthier path to success. Do not ignore what may be going on inside you while you're trying to go through a change. You will find that opening up to a trusted person and talking through what you are going through helps create closure and frees you to move on to the next phase with more confidence. As you look at the future with encouragement, it also reminds you of why you are going through the change.

When change comes your way, here are some typical emotions you may feel:

- Fear
- Sadness
- Unsafe
- Unhappy
- A sense of loss, etc.

- Anger
- Denial
- Frustrated
- Sick

Stage 2: The neutral zone

This zone is where you are getting used to the change that is happening. You are learning new ways of doing things and can expect the learning curve here to be stressful. You'll need to remind yourself as you go between the love and hate period that you are still making progress because you are slowly adapting to the change—even if it does not feel that way.

In this stage, you may notice the following reactions:

- You may struggle with your identity because you feel unsure of how to do things. When you begin to struggle with your identity, remember to seek help and go through the steps in Chapter 2.
- You may become skeptical about the change and find yourself harking-back. Regaining your focus will help you if you find yourself in this situation, and the 4Rs in chapter 1 is a good resource.
- Frustration will kick in if you don't see results right away. This drains your motivation and energy. You may begin to procrastinate and put off the necessary work you had mapped out for yourself.

The best way to approach this stage is to be both persistent and consistent, remaining focused on your crystal-clear goals and the path you are on. Find positive affirmations for motivation and encouragement. Surround yourself with the right support and fill your mind with positive vibes, holding strong to the vision of your success.

Arm yourself with the knowledge that what worked before in previous situations may not work in a new one. Organize yourself to learn about the adventure (figuring out what to learn, from whom to learn it, and how best to accelerate the learning process around culture, language, and systems). Just as mentioned earlier, just because you have a hammer, you cannot treat everything as a nail when the job may need a drill. As a woman, you know that, depending on where you are going, you may need a different set of items in your handbag along with the basic necessities that are always there.

Lastly, be sure to celebrate the little wins on your journey—don't wait to celebrate only the big ones. This is because celebrating accomplishments will boost your morale. On the other hand, as you go along, look out for any roadblocks that may be killing motivation and do your best to eliminate them. Be patient with yourself, knowing that change is a learning process, and you will make it through if you just persist.

Stage 3: The new beginning

We immigrated to Canada as a family of six, including four young children, and it was a trying period. The weather was freezing, the snow was knee-deep, the days were shorter, and it was challenging to find a job that paid reasonably. We had a double stroller and no car. Every time I pushed that double stroller on those snowy footpaths, I questioned the sanity of our decision to come to Canada.

We grew more anxious as we had more financial outflows than inflows. My husband started a transitional job, and it came with challenges of its own. Just as he started feeling very strongly that it wasn't too late to turn back, I quickly forgot my own worries and focused on supporting him. As with every new beginning, we suddenly realized one day that we were okay. My husband had started a good job, we had a car, the kids and I were settled, and things were finally falling into place.

Do you recognize moments like this in your own journey? Where the trying times fade imperceptibly, and everything falls into place? This is the "new beginning" stage of the Bridges Transitional Model, and it is where you begin to see the results of the change and the journey. You see the new way as being better than the old way, and you are a shining success. Hurray! All your efforts have paid off, and you are now effortlessly living your new life.

- You feel positive,
- You become more committed to the dream, desire, and journey,
- You are energized and on fire for the cause, and
- You are willing and ready to do more and learn more.

This stage is where you celebrate. You have just begun your success journey, and the strategies we will explore in the coming chapters will help you sustain the best direction for your journey.

Action:

- Open your journal or notebook.
- Complete the "life map" and "shape your path" exercises.

• Make a list of ways to celebrate all the milestones at each step of your journey. Just like with your life map, you can theme your celebrations and rewards. For example, when I finished my professional exam, I binge-watched movies as my reward because I had not watched movies while studying and juggling life. When I did my first five-kilometer run for charity, I booked a massage as a reward because I'd trained for months to ensure my success. The reward or celebration can be big or small, but it is really important to make sure you have a list of rewards ready to help you celebrate each milestone. It's motivating and something to look forward to.

Recap

Shaping your path is serious business. You do not want to be on a journey and get to the end of it only to discover you have been on the wrong path the whole time. In this chapter, I have outlined three important messages to help you successfully bridge the gap between where you are and where you want to be—and the bridge is literally the metaphoric transition you are going through. Transitions are different from change and are more challenging because they involve internal reactions to an external change. These internal reactions require transformational life changes that involve ending old ways of doing things and embracing new ways of life.

• **What is your story, and how does it guide your journey?** The life map exercise is based on the concept of the impact our stories have in our lives—or how they direct them. There are many stories in your life. The stories around important events direct any future decisions you make, but you may or may not be aware of them. Using the life map exercise, you are able to know and understand your story and can use that knowledge to focus the rest of your journey toward success.

• **Transition planning to shape your path.** To get to your destination, you need to be aware of who is in charge. When using the analogy of going on a bus trip, we reflected on who or what is directing your life, and more importantly, if your life is going in the direction you wanted it to.

We discussed that the driver has complete control of the journey. They navigate the detours, the speed bumps, and they control the speed of the bus. On the other hand, being the passenger leaves our life to chance, although, depending on the situation, we may influence the driver.

To successfully get to your desired destination with minimal stress, you will want to be the driver! We discussed ways to take charge if you need to, with the first step being answering the "shaping-your-path pre-planning guide".

• **The three Stages of the Bridges Transition Model:** There is a gap between where you currently are and where you want to be. This model provides the bridge between the two.

By using it, you can master your transition process by understanding that what you are going through at any stage is normal.

The three stages include:

(a) The ending, which involves letting go so that you are prepared to start the new journey,

(b) The neutral zone, which is a struggle between the old ways and the new ways that have already begun, and

(c) The new beginnings where you are now enjoying the results of the change.

Fun fact: My key is on a green keychain inscribed with the Bible verse from Ecclesiastes 3:11 that reads: "He makes all things beautiful in his time." The keys I carry in my handbag symbolize that I am steering the wheels of my journey in the direction of the Holy Spirit, who assures me that all things will be beautiful. What reminds you of who is in charge of your life?

Congratulations! You have mastered the foundational strategies for successful transition and transformational change. Be reminded that the act of immigrating induces many life lessons. You cannot afford to waste this opportunity that life as an immigrant has presented to you.

Part 2 lays out the strategies you need to sustain the successful results of your new beginnings.

PART 2

Mind the Gap

"Ideals of reason tell us how the world should be; experience tells us that it rarely is. Growing up involves confronting the gap between the two without giving up on either one."
—Susan Neiman

In part one, you spent some time mapping out your journey to ensure your success. As you embark on an adventure, or if you are already on one, you must be crystal clear about where you are going and why. You must know yourself and have a roadmap and a transition plan that clearly identify who is in charge. However, it would not be prudent to stop there as there is a need to sustain the successful start of your new beginning.

Hurdles and Bridges

"It is not the strongest of the species that survives, nor the most intelligent that survives. It is the one that is most adaptable to change." —Charles Darwin

While on any journey—big or small—difficulties and challenges arise. These challenges can have a significant impact on you and your entire journey. Not only could they be costly in terms of finances, but also in terms of your time, energy, and emotions. Your swift response to these challenges could minimize such impacts.

One key to minimizing the impacts of unforeseen challenges is being properly prepared.

The power of anticipating challenges

"Sensible people will see trouble coming and avoid it, but an unthinking person will walk right into it and regret it later." —Proverbs 22:3 (Good News Translation)

A plan that does not consider challenges and only celebrates wins is bound to fail.

Do you know why I am proud of immigrant women? I believe we are already experts in the skill of adaptability. How else could you uproot yourself from a life that is full of knowns and embrace another with more uncertainties than you can think of? You would already have done a lot of scenario planning before you set out. And if you didn't, then I hope this book has illustrated how important it is to do so.

I have an emergency kit[7] in the trunk of my car. The kit has all kinds of things in it, including booster cables, flashlights, reflective blankets, granola bars, nuts, water, etc. The kit can keep you safe in case of an emergency because you never know when or where emergencies will happen. My emergency kit sometimes feels like unnecessary baggage, but because I usually have my children with me, I'd rather be prepared for any eventuality.

Anticipating challenges is not the same as dwelling on negatives or beating yourself up over problems that may come up in a situation you have intentionally put yourself in. No! It's about being proactive and taking charge.

A study in the Motivation and Emotions journal[8] states that anticipating what may go wrong helps people to "close the gap between wanting to attain a goal and attaining it."

What do you do when change occurs? The reality is that if you do not adapt, you will be left behind. One good example in the business world is BlackBerry. BlackBerry was once the superpower of smartphones. BlackBerry, however, crashed because it failed to innovate. It was not anticipating changes in the smartphone industry, so it did nothing different, and thus, the iPhone and other Android smartphones took over the market.

Ask yourself questions such as what do I need to anticipate? How is my journey going to change? Most times, we tend to react quickly to changes. This is called agility. Agility is a great skill; however, I'd like you to consider this question asked by Daniel Burrus in his book, *The Anticipatory Organization: Turn Disruption and Change Into Opportunity and Advantage.*

---

7 http://www.aema.alberta.ca/documents/emergency-vehicle-checklist.pdf
8 Gollwitzer, P.M. Weakness of the will: Is a quick fix possible? Motiv Emot 38, 305–322 (2014). https://doi.org/10.1007/s11031-014-9416-3

"Would you rather have merely reacted as quickly as possible as change took place, or anticipated it and crafted well-thought-out plans to take advantage of its game-changing opportunities?"

I certainly, would rather anticipate the change, plan for it, and be ready to take advantage of the opportunities that the change presents.

This is the major advantage of anticipating challenges. It puts you ahead of the curve and creates opportunities you may not otherwise have seen.

In summary:
- Change is the only constant.
- Change brings challenges.
- Change brings opportunities.
- To survive in an ever-changing world with many challenges and opportunities, you need to be adaptable and innovative to succeed.

As Burrus says in his book, when you adopt an anticipatory mindset, you learn <u>not</u> to focus on your competition. When you focus on your competition, you will be tempted to adopt what they do and look like them. So, instead of imitating, you learn to innovate by intentionally focusing on what the competition is *not* doing. Because of her level of exposure to change, challenges, and different experiences, an immigrant woman is well-positioned to innovate instead of imitating what others are doing.

"What-if... then" planning, a.k.a. scenario planning

How does one anticipate challenges?

Anticipating challenges should not become a journey into the negativity zone. Rather, you should consider what road-blocks you may encounter and plan out different scenarios to make sure your journey doesn't have to come to a stop or be diverted off-course. Earlier, we talked about how expensive that could be for you. Planning scenarios can be a fun yet serious exercise if you understand the goal of the exercise.

The future is not likely to be just like the past. I grew up without cell phones and apps. I also remember how we could just burst into our friends and neighbors' homes, running in and out at will without any worries that something "bad" may happen. These days, we have a new definition of safety to work with—think about cyber security and the increasing rate of mental health issues. Though there are many things one cannot simply predict, as pointed out in Proverbs 22:3, it will still be folly to think things will remain as they currently are.

For an immigrant woman, it becomes more important to anticipate what could be five, ten, or fifteen years from now. Not having a strong strategy that looks ahead can be disas-trous because it does not give a new beginning enough time to fully take off. If you do not consider what the new begin-ning may look like, or at least consider that the environment may be different from what it currently is when your dream is fully hatched, you might find yourself in a constant state of starting afresh.

Scenario planning provides a structured framework for evaluating the links between what is known today and what could happen tomorrow.

Scenario planning is the secret to adapting. Many businesses have been using this tool with success for years, and you can also use it. It's an item to have in your handbag as you go through life.

Shell, for instance, has been developing scenarios of the future since the 1970s. They describe its value on their website as follows:

"Shell Scenarios[9] ask "what if?" questions, encouraging leaders to consider events that may only be remote possibilities and stretch their thinking." Shell's view on the value of scenario planning is that "Good scenarios explore the possible, not just the probable—providing a relevant challenge to the conventional wisdom of their users and helping them prepare for the major changes ahead. They will provide a useful context for debate, leading to better policy and strategy, and a shared understanding of, and commitment to, actions."

When there is change in your life, challenges are bound to happen. It is, therefore, imperative for you as an immigrant woman often to ponder events and scenarios that might occur in your journey and consider how you would manage them should they materialize. Preparing multiple "what if … then" scenarios will nudge you to take actions that will be beneficial tomorrow.

I think of scenario planning as akin to doing my estate planning. Just like change, death (and taxes) is certain. Scenario planning helps you focus on what is important and what matters most, instead of reacting and responding to crises and putting out fires.

9 https://www.shell.com/energy-and-innovation/the-energy-future/scenarios.html

Getting started with scenario planning

In the next three chapters, we will explore some challenges that most immigrant women face on their journey, and the following two ideas will get you going on scenario planning.

1. Brainstorming and research

First, brainstorm and identify all the factors that are causing challenges in the present and those likely to cause challenges in the future. Some you may not even have considered yet. One immigrant woman I interviewed recalled some of the challenges she'd faced as a tourist. Then she reminded herself that there was a big difference between being a tourist and an immigrant, namely:

- A tourist is on a shorter trip in a new country than an immigrant is.
- A tourist has a familiar way of life that they won't need to adjust to on their return from their trip.
- A tourist tends to spend more "fun" money on their trip because that is part of the plan, while, on the other hand, an immigrant is living their everyday life, and finances can be a problem.

Armed with this knowledge, she compiled some likely challenges she might face as an immigrant, as well as those she had faced as a tourist. She also asked around to learn what others might have heard or gone through. What was preventing people from achieving their dreams? Were there any workarounds they could share? From their experience and knowledge, what situations might occur in the future? What would they do if this happened?

These days, there's so much information available on social media that it's a lot easier to learn about what people are undergoing and gain a sense of what may be lining up for the future.

Collect all these possible scenarios. Feel free to write them down as stories or "business proposals" should any materialize.

2. Desired outcome

After you have gathered a few scenarios, the next step would be to determine some actions you could take if any of them should happen. This process can help you anticipate and overcome challenges before they take place.

Remember the woman in the first step who brainstormed some challenges she faced as a tourist as well as other possible situations she was not yet aware of? For step two, she took a rather simple action from one of the scenarios she had drawn up. Focusing on a situation where she might not immediately find a well-paying job during her transition, she picked one expense to save for so that she need not worry about it for a year. In this case, she saved enough to stock up on her toiletries for one full year. This way, if she spent that long doing a low-paying transition job, she could focus on meeting her basic needs of food and shelter as she settled in, i.e., she would not need to worry about her personal hygiene, which is an important part of self-care.

Tip: When I am planning scenarios, I make the process fun by writing them as compelling stories and proposals. The viable actions and knowledge I have gained in the process become the foundation for potential projects and initiatives as I go along on my journey.

Before we move into further exploration of some challenges and winning strategies, it is important to remember that you are not trying to make the future perfect or consider everything that could go wrong. You are simply using your imagination and creativity to set yourself up to be ahead of the game as a successful immigrant woman.

To close, scenario planning:

- Will lessen negative outcomes and events that may derail you,
- Will help you confidently navigate challenges, and
- Will open opportunities you may not have noticed before.

Through scenario planning, you acknowledge that the future cannot be predicted but that you can be prepared by taking proactive action.

"A person may plan his own journey, but the LORD directs his steps." —Proverbs 16:9 (God's Word Translation).

In the chapters that follow, you will be well equipped with strategies to overcome the challenges that come with big life changes. You will also be reminded of the many reasons to be grateful in your journey.

CHAPTER 4

Broadening Your Horizons

"There are no foreign lands. It is the traveler only who is foreign." —Robert Louis Stevenson

As a kid, I was convinced my mom had eyes at the back of her head. She seemed to know everything, including things that happened in her absence. I think every child thinks that. As an adult, you may know this is not true, but I can tell you that when I was growing up, to me, it really was true.

Our moms and dads did have eyes, not only at the back of their heads but everywhere. I had so many aunties and uncles growing up that it was almost impossible to do anything without someone seeing me and telling my parents. In Nigeria, where I grew up, you had to refer to anyone older than you by at least ten years as uncle or aunty. And if they were old enough to be your grandparents, then they were your grandparents.

Of course, when we had our children, we also introduced anyone older than my husband or me as aunty or uncle. The first time a friend introduced herself to my young son by her first name, I was quick to add "aunty" and tell my son to use that term. Well, it did not take long for me to realize that I was fighting a losing battle because, in Italy, everyone introduced themselves on a first-name basis. This was new and strange to me. For the longest time, I felt that not referring to these people as aunty and uncle was disrespectful. However, like many other things, that feeling wore off with time.

Welcome to culture shock!

Shock doesn't sound pleasant, and nor does culture shock. There's no way to prepare for it. Every immigrant must experience it, and no amount of preparation will prevent it from happening. It is normal and to be expected, but it can have a positive impact on your life.

Being aware of culture shock and knowing some of the things you can do in any specific season will help you navigate this period, and you will come out of it stronger.

What is shock? According to Dictionary.com[10], a shock is a sudden upsetting or surprising event or experience. Our bodies will react in many physiological ways, including widening our eyes, pumping our heart faster, suddenly breaking out in a cold sweat, shivering constantly. Sometimes certain kinds of shock can lead to death.

Culture shock is not much different from any other kind of shock. It is usually sudden (no matter how much you expected it), and it can be an upsetting experience. According

---

10 https://www.lexico.com/definition/shock

to Dictionary.com[11], **culture shock** is a state of bewilderment and distress experienced by an individual who is suddenly exposed to a new, strange, or foreign social and cultural environment.

What does culture shock look like?

Culture shock comes in many forms, and people experience it in varying degrees. When culture shock strikes, it either hits you right away or slowly eats at you. Regardless, it leaves you feeling anxious, nervous, confused, overwhelmed, disgusted, angry, and homesick. Basically, culture shock is caused by stress due to exposure to a new culture. This is because culture runs deep. It is and has been your way of doing things for your entire lifetime. Therefore, learning new ways of going about life is a massive endeavor, and it's no surprise that it will cause a tremendous amount of stress.

Consider some of these examples and how you may react to them.

Food culture shock:

> *"Food is not rational. Food is culture, habit, craving and identity." —Jonathan Safran Foer*

After a few months in our new home, I took a part-time transition job as a cashier at a concession food store. I learned things about the culture from our customers, who taught me about food, cowboy/cowgirl clothes, and how to make small talk!

---

11 https://www.dictionary.com/browse/culture-shock#:~:text=a%20state%20of%20bewilderment%20and,foreign%20social%20and%20cultural%20environment.

I take yet another order as I mutter a quick prayer under my breath. Every eight-hour shift slowly turns into a nightmare.

"Poutine, please!" one customer says nicely.

"Fish and chips," comes another gruff request.

And then someone else says in a rather high-pitched voice, "Chicken strips and corn dogs."

The cashiers are bustling, attending to the lineup of customers, there to watch a derby, which is a type of horse race. The smell of fatty, fried food drifts in from the kitchen behind us as we yell out the food orders to the kitchen staff.

I stare at the order in my hand as I wonder what sauce goes with what. The chef is getting frustrated with the number of times I have to throw out food because, once again, I have put the wrong sauce on something.

One day, I finally broke down. I couldn't take it anymore, and I asked to be properly educated on these foods because I had never seen or heard of them before.

The food of their host country is a common shock to people from different places. Before you go to a new place, do some research to see what kinds of food may be available. If you are a guest and your host offers you something you are not familiar with, make sure you know what manners are appropriate, and do not do or say anything that will be seen as disrespectful.

Role culture shock

As social beings, our identities are closely tied to our roles. As a simple example, I identify as a mother, but motherhood can be categorized as a role I play and not really my identity. One of the biggest impacts of immigrating with young children was role shock. When we arrived in Canada, the first available work was "survival" or transition jobs, and they did not pay well. Up to the point of our immigration, we were a single-income family and comfortable financially.

However, on our arrival in Canada, this arrangement was disrupted by unfamiliar expectations. Just as I identified as a mother, the self-concept and identity of most men are dependent on their social roles, interpersonal relationships, and wellbeing. For my husband, the change in his social role as a well-established, skilled person to a new, unfamiliar role in a transition job was inconsistent with his identity. This caused him a great deal of stress, which hung over the entire household during that period. This, in turn, led me to start searching for part-time transition jobs, including night shifts, so we could always have a parent with the children and avoid the cost of childcare.

It was a major disruption to our way of living, our plans, and family values. It was a big relief when my husband was able to find work that was aligned with his skills and career path. Adjusting expectations and having a supportive network go a long way in managing role shock.

Time culture shock

> *"The stranger sees only what he knows."*
> —*African proverb, Author Unknown*

When I compare time through my Nigerian lens, it almost feels as if we have more than twenty-four hours in Nigeria. Time is slow compared to North America. In fact, you may have heard of "African time". Some people use this as a negative way to mean that certain people are lazy. However, when I reflect on my days in Nigeria, I was productive even though the approach to time is different. Most of the people I worked with were not lazy or disrespectful either; rather, it was simply a way of life that was part of our culture.

That said, I remember feeling out of breath when going places in Canada as a newcomer. I was always "racing", even while walking. This caused me a lot of anxiety because I would leave early to have ample time to travel at my slower pace. Other times, I was worried that I might be late or out of breath. The simple thought of going someplace important impacted my mental wellness and other behavior. It was not a good feeling.

Later, I learned about monochronic and polychronic time cultures, and I realized nothing was wrong with me or my "shorter strides". This awareness built my confidence, and I no longer beat myself up for appearing tardy when, in fact, I was not. It was just a perception I'd had when I thought something was wrong with me. This lesson is important because under-standing why we do what we do and knowing that no culture is superior helps us celebrate our differences and similarities.

I've elaborated on monochronic and polychronic time cultures below because the concept has a far-reaching impact on how you communicate and present yourself when people from different cultures are around.

Monochronic culture: In places where things are typi-cally done one at a time and time is scheduled, arranged, and managed, a monochronic culture sees time linearly. In such a culture, time is viewed as a tangible commodity that can be spent, saved, or wasted. Value is placed on schedules, tasks, and "getting the job done". This perception of time is rooted in the Industrial Revolution of the eighteenth and nineteenth centuries, and the examples of cultures that are monochronic include the United States, Germany, Switzerland, Britain, Canada, Japan, South Korea, Turkey, and the Scandinavian countries.

Polychronic culture: In this type of culture, several things can be done at once. The approach to scheduling time is more fluid. Time is seen more through relationships and traditions, not just tasks. In the days of my grandma, time was not based on clocks or calendars but on seasons, religious and cultural festivals, sunrises and sunsets, or when animals woke up and went to sleep. Many Latin American, African, Asian, and Arab cultures fall into this category, for example, countries like Mexico, Pakistan, India, rural China, the Philippines, Egypt, and Saudi Arabia.

Other culture shock examples include body language and accent, dressing styles, giving tips for services received, etc.

You are sure to go through one or more of these and many other kinds of culture shock when immigrating. Again, adjusting to a new culture is a gradual process and takes time, so give yourself the space and time to adjust. Seek help when needed. Most host countries have lots of resources to help immigrants integrate and adapt. We will explore how you can use your culture shock experiences to thrive in any new situation.

Symptoms of culture shock

When an immigrant begins to ask questions like "What have I gotten myself into?", "What am I doing here?", "What is the matter with these people?", and "Why can't they do it the right way?" you can be pretty sure that some degree of transition shock is happening. Generally, you may find yourself comparing your current life with what worked before in a negative way. This is Harking-Back.

Symptoms of culture shock vary from person to person. Most are similar to other reactions that occur day-to-day. This makes it easy to dismiss, deny or ignore culture shock when it's happening and sometimes to shift the blame onto other people. Sometimes it's not as easy to recognize as you might think, as it's a little more complicated than having a case of "bad days". It's also worth noting that if you feel any number of these below, they can be caused by many other reasons not related to culture shock.

I think one of the worst things about culture shock is that most people bear these pains alone. You don't know who to talk to and if you will be understood. There are no groups to join, and people aren't sharing their experiences. Frankly, I never even heard of culture shock until a few years ago when I started working with international students. Knowing that culture shock is inevitable and not unusual was an encouragement, and it can help you build confidence that this is a normal reaction to immigration.

Common symptoms of culture shock:

- **Homesickness and sadness:**
  This is a common one for most people. I find this comes and goes, even after several years. And after living outside of Nigeria for a few decades now, there are times I long for my home country very badly. Sometimes it's triggered by the season; at other times, it's an experience or a memory.

  Christmas time is one of those moments. Whenever I have that nostalgic feeling for the good old days, I recognize what I am feeling, and I laugh or cry about it, then move on. This nostalgia reminds me to create memorable traditions and experiences for my children, family, and friends so that if they, too, ever long for home, they will have good memories to carry them through. It also reminds me to be kind to those I meet who may be feeling homesick as well.

• **Feelings of helplessness and dependency:** It can be quite demoralizing when you feel you don't know enough about your new environment to make decisions for yourself or contribute in a meaningful way. You feel helpless, and at times, lost. You may have to go with other people's decisions because you don't know how things work and who to trust.

This is a disempowering situation, and any immigrant woman can feel like this at any point in her journey, regardless of her education, socio-economic status, etc. When I come across such a situation, one thing that always works for me is to find and join a support group. This could be online, in the local library, or by reaching out to trusted contacts.

Volunteering also provides an outlet that can make you feel you are being helpful and/or having an impact. Volunteering helps refocus your mind on giving to other people, and thus, away from your problems. And potentially, you could gain valuable information from people you meet through your volunteer engagements.

• **Disorientation and isolation:**
Have you ever been surrounded by many people, yet you have this feeling of being all alone? Loneliness is an ache in the heart that is hard to describe because it's so different from physical pain. Many months

of my first immigration experience were filled with feelings of isolation and disorientation.

The only person I knew back then was my husband. I didn't speak the language, and I was pregnant with our first child. There was a lot happening all at once. I remember thinking back then that I could return to my workplace in Nigeria since I had not yet formally quit my job. Rather, I had chosen to take a three-month leave of absence and still had my return ticket.

Honestly, I do not know how I got through this period. I believe it was the gift of my pregnancy that saved me. As I had to be in good shape for my baby, I took numerous walks around the neighborhood. This not only provided me with an opportunity to get some fresh air and move about, but it was also a way to see other people and smile.

• **Inappropriate anger and hostility**:
I once had an encounter with a single immigrant mother at my workplace. She came in to see me because no one else wanted to work with her. Less than two minutes into our interaction, it was easy to see why. She came off as brash and rude. I was intrigued by that because she needed help, but she was not helping her case.

I chose to ignore her attitude and behavior and instead listened for the underlying issues. As I listened to her, I realized she was putting up a front to protect herself and her children from the fears and insecurity that she was experiencing as an immigrant woman. As soon as I discovered what was going on inside her, I was better able to empathize with her. I further coached and supported her in acquiring resources that would help her to feel a sense of safety for her children and herself.

Over time, it was amazing to see the confident and successful woman she became, not to mention that she now pays it forward by supporting other single moms.

• Sleep and eating disturbances (too little or too much): When we are worried and feel unsafe, we indulge in different coping mechanisms. These vary among individuals. Some of these coping mechanisms can be negative, some positive. For some of us, culture shock impacts our energy levels, and this may result in finding ways to comfort ourselves—or we just bury our heads and believe that the feeling will soon go away.

Food and sleep are comforting for most people. On the other hand, when you're anxious, it may be challenging to sleep well or eat well. If you are going through periods of low energy, being able to identify the cause is a big step to dealing with the problem. When my energy is low, I think of those things that energize me, and I engage in them. For example, I love to listen to Christian music. I also love to read. So, instead of sleeping too much or too little or overindulging in unhealthy eating habits, which would ultimately worsen my situation, I listen to some music, sing and dance, or grab a book and start to read.

These simple acts are like magic to my energy levels. So, figure out what fills your energy tank and use that to support yourself when you feel low.

• Anxiety over health and safety:

When we moved to Canada, I noticed that many homes had light curtains and blinds, and as a result, I could see the inside of people's homes to varying degrees. I felt that people's homes should be private, not exposed, and that bothered me.

I felt unsafe in our rented house, which was furnished with see-through curtains, as I imagined criminals would be able to see inside our home and harm us. This view was based on my experience of life in Nigeria, where we lived in houses with tall, gated fences.

I was under a great deal of anxiety day and night during those first few months, and it took a while to feel safe with the large windows and see-through blinds. I was finally able to adjust to this level of exposure when I asked myself what was true about this situation. I looked into reports on criminal activity in the area and discovered that since we had moved into that house, there was not one case reported. That helped me finally to accept this change and relax.

Thoughts are powerful. They influence our beliefs and can cause us to take certain actions. Thus, by capturing any untrue thoughts, I can tame my anxiety. So, whenever I feel anxious, I use the acronym TRUE, and I ask myself the following questions:

T–is this True?

R–is this Right?

U–is this Undeniable?

E–is this Excellent?

I made this acronym from the following scripture that commands us about our thoughts. *"And now, dear brothers and sisters, one final thing. Fix your thoughts on what is true, and honorable, and right, and pure, and lovely, and admirable. Think about things that are excellent and worthy of praise."* — Philippians 4:8 (New Living Translation).

I share these TRUE questions with my children and friends when they are anxious. It helps to put things in perspective while calming apprehensive thoughts and feelings.

Stages of culture shock

Part of recognizing culture shock includes being aware of its causes and symptoms and phases.

There are four primary phases of culture shock. These phases are both sequential and cyclical. As new experiences and culture shock present themselves, you may find you shift from crisis to adjustment, then onto adaptation.

Within a few months of arriving in Canada, I was fortunate to enroll in a pilot program that provided internationally trained accountants an opportunity to get their professional licenses in Canada. The program was intended to provide support while they worked on professional accounting training, exams, and designation.

All the candidates were seasoned practicing accountants from different parts of the world who had recently immigrated to Canada. I had not yet been exposed to any literature or education around culture shock, but it was here that I saw firsthand the rawness of it. The men and women in my class went through the different phases of culture shock in various degrees. Though we could relate to each other's experiences, the highs and lows were individual.

Unfortunately, after the initial pilot, this program was not continued. Less than half of the pilot participants were successful in challenging the exams. This was because there were too many adjustments to make, including language barriers, the need to sustain their finances, unfamiliar weather, differences in education style, etc. I believe that, among other factors, my experiences from our first immigration venture helped me succeed.

Being more aware, I now cringe at the stress we were all under as we worked on achieving our dreams and establishing ourselves in a new country. We could have dealt with many problems more effectively if only we had known about culture shock. Yes, culture shock is real and highlights some negative experiences; however, what you are learning from this book will set you up for success. I have listed some powerful strategies to include in your handbag as you move along through your life journey.

The four phases of culture shock are:
1. The honeymoon phase,
2. The crisis or culture shock phase,
3. The adjustment phase, and
4. The adaptation phase.

The honeymoon phase

This can be likened to how a tourist or someone vacationing feels about a new place. You fall in love with it. You find yourself in awe of everything, including the sounds and sights. You will excuse things that may have irritated you, even in your own culture. While you might experience some anxiety or stress, you will perceive it positively. This phase is characterized by excitement, interest, euphoria, sleeplessness, positive expectations, and idealization of the host culture. But like every honeymoon, this high will come to an end, so this phase does not last very long.

The crisis or culture shock phase

This phase hits people differently and may start gradually or as a full-blown crisis. It may also present as a series of escalating problems and negative experiences. Depending on the individual, their level of preparation, and other factors, the shift from honeymoon to crisis phase usually happens within a few days to a few weeks.

In this stage, minor things can become major issues, and cultural differences are irritating. Though people's reactions are different, it is characterized by increasing frustrations, disappointments, and feelings of helplessness and confusion. The loss of control could lead to depression, and high emotional swings may cause extreme fatigue and physical illness. It's at this stage that some people just want to go back home.

The adjustment phase

Thankfully, the crisis phase will eventually pass, and those who did not go home during the culture shock phase may do one of two things. Some, unfortunately, adopt various forms of isolation, living in an ethnic enclave, and avoid learning about the new culture. Needless to say, this attitude further shrinks opportunities for meaningful success. On the other hand, others may begin to accept that they need to see and do things differently to adjust to their new environment.

To function effectively and successfully, it's important to adapt by developing problem-solving skills to deal with cultural differences in positive ways. During the adjustment phase, your problems do not go away; however, you are open to learning the new culture. Your reactions are positive because you now know that your problems came from not understanding how things work.

A positive appreciation of the new culture begins to emerge as you adjust and start to adapt. At this stage, your positive attitude to problem-solving helps you to see your challenges in a different light and addressing them becomes more fun than pain.

The adaptation phase

In the adaptation phase, you adapt to some cultural differences. These adaptations help you as an immigrant woman to successfully navigate life and solve problems. During this phase, you will notice that you have undergone a substantial personal change and may even be developing a bicultural identity. Bicultural identity as defined in the *Encyclopedia of Child Behavior and Development* as "the acceptance of both the dominant and home cultures that is within an individual's identity."[12] You can now embrace values from the host and home cultures and engage in positive intercultural exchange.

You will feel empowered by all these experiences and will notice substantial personal change due to your cultural adaptation. It is important to recognize and accept that you have changed. Your self-concept with the development of a

12 https://link.springer.com/
referenceworkentry/10.1007%2F978-0-387-79061-9_331

bicultural identity is not negative; rather, it means you have integrated new cultural aspects into your existing ones. As an immigrant woman, this gives you an advantage because your approach to problem-solving will be more robust and holistic. Your experience will also help you empathize with people going through similar challenges.

Culture shock therapy

"There is wisdom in turning as often as possible from the familiar to the unfamiliar: it keeps the mind nimble; it kills prejudice and it fosters humor."
—George Santayana, *Philosophy of Travel*

Meaningful growth happens when we step out of our comfort zone and take risks. Whether you know it or not, you, as an immigrant, are already shaking things up by your courageous act of embarking on a new journey. Since culture shock is a normal phenomenon and totally unavoidable for any immigrant, why not harness it to your advantage? Why not see this experience as a big learning curve in your life journey, and apply the techniques and strategies you used during the phases of culture shock to guide you whenever you face any change, big or small? After all, if you've read this far, these strategies are already in your handbag, a confident and empowering bundle ready to be used.

Managing your culture shock experience is fundamental to success

According to the Cambridge English Dictionary, therapy is a treatment that helps someone feel better, grow stronger, etc., especially after an illness. Culture shock is not an illness, but it has a tremendous impact on the emotional wellbeing of people. Just like people join clubs and associations as therapy for loneliness or to establish support systems after a loss or through something they are battling with, one can benefit from being exposed to culture shock.

Here's a tested approach that I and some of the successful immigrant women I've worked with have used. It effectively manages culture shock, whether it has occurred because of personal life change, organizational change, or travel.

1. Understand that culture shock is normal. As discussed earlier, when undergoing culture shock, you may not easily recognize it. This is because the symptoms can also be mistaken for other ailments.
2. Recognize culture shock. Being aware of what is causing you problems and naming it goes a long way toward solving problems and managing them.
3. Implement behaviors to overcome culture shock with balanced changes. Openness and acceptance of the new culture will help you adapt to it. You do not need to become someone else; you can be yourself and know how to immerse yourself in the new culture with less stress.
4. An effective technique that sums up what I have said above is to recognize culture shock, reframe the situation by adapting your responses, and make use of problem-solving strategies.

Adaptation strategies

The goal of adaptation is not to lose your culture or identity but to begin immersing yourself in the new culture.

• Planning ahead and researching the culture of your destination before setting out helps most people to adjust effectively and faster. However, not everyone has access to resources that allow for pre-planning. Therefore, if you cannot do any pre-planning, it is important to know that there's always help available elsewhere. In the case of immigration, many host countries have immigrant services to support you. These organizations offer a ton of resources, and one of their initial goals is to help newcomers stabilize and become quickly integrated into their new place. There are also counselors, therapists, and coaches who can support and guide you through change. Lastly, the importance of your social support network cannot be over-emphasized. Immersing yourself in a new culture requires you to get out of your comfort zone and join groups that are different from those in your culture. This will broaden your knowledge of the new culture.

• Reframing your situation through the lens of the new culture is a game-changer. Often, when faced with a situation, people are quick to revert to old processes and solutions. While these may have worked in a different environment, they may not work in the new one. With the information you have acquired from the pre-planning process, you can reframe your experience and may be able to see new ways to approach the situation. Reframing problems fosters tolerance of the new culture and leads away from negative reactions.

• It is also important to recognize that while trying to adapt, your physical needs must still be met. If there are issues around food, shelter, health, and/or general wellness, it will be challenging to focus on adaptation strategies. The goal here is to stabilize first. This will involve finding transition jobs and resources. In this situation, I highly recommend working with immigrant service organizations as the stress of not meeting basic needs intensifies culture shock.

• Lastly, I would again highlight the importance of social support networks. They will eliminate a lot of stressors while having a direct impact on how you effectively manage culture shock. They also help with cultural adaptation by validating your sense of self-worth. This is achieved through affirmation, acceptance, and assurance, as well as giving you opportunities for venting your emotions. All these lead to a better understanding of stressful situations (Adelman, 1988).[13]

• Social support networks can be close ties like family and friends or weaker ties such as church, neighbors, and acquaintances. Organizations such as clubs, immigrant services, schools, sports teams, and community associations provide a platform for social interactions. These interactions help with learning verbal and non-verbal language while also offering other opportunities through intercultural mingling and adaptation. These social support groups will help you to build trusted relationships with people of your culture and those of other cultures, which in turn will broaden your horizons and help eliminate culture shock.

13 Mara B. Adelman, "Cross-Cultural Adjustment," *International Journal of Intercultural Relations* 12, no. 3 (1988): pp. 183-204, https://doi.org/10.1016/0147-1767(88)90015-6.

The blooming impact of culture shock

"When a caterpillar becomes a butterfly, it takes all of its experiences and everything that lives inside itself and transforms into a beautiful creature. What people don't always notice is the metamorphosis—the isolation, the discomfort, even the pain." —Terryca Taylor,
Memoirs of a Butterfly: Letters to a Caterpillar.

Since culture shock is normal, it can be empowering when you embrace the experience with positivity. It gives you an opportunity to learn about yourself, it teaches you how to think on your feet and adapt, and it enables you to immerse yourself in an entirely new culture to emerge as a global citizen.

Every experience you have is meant to teach you something! Here are a few things that happen when you learn from culture shock:

1. **Tremendous personal growth:** Being in an unfamiliar place makes you vulnerable, and it's in this vulnerability that you truly discover who you are and what innate gifts you have. In the scary, confusing moments when you reach your lowest points and hit rock bottom, the only way to move is up. Culture shock teaches you survival skills as you learn to "trust your gut" in those lonely moments. This is where your character, the true "you" will be exposed, and it offers you the chance to build and refine that character. In my journey as an immigrant woman, it's in those moments where I have met the barriers of cultural differences that I have chosen to be the voice of other immigrant women, whether that be as a school council member, a board member, or the lector in the church

that embraces my accent and looks. I speak up with confidence.

2 Expand your thinking: Immersing yourself in a new culture and learning to use the language in real-life situations outside the classroom is a big deal. A lot of people don't stop to think about it. Immigrants are expected to learn the language and the culture, and when they are slow, some people in their host culture tend to be frustrated with them. Learning a new language requires a lot of thought and energy.

Standing on your feet and interacting day by day with a new language and in a new culture is accomplished by the need to think differently. Sometimes we think that language involves only spoken words, but it's the unspoken words that make up more than seventy percent of language. To adjust effectively and adapt successfully, an immigrant woman must understand and interpret the body language of other cultures, such as hand and facial gestures. And to make matters worse, there's the added pressure that this understanding is expected. It is a one-way relationship; however, the immigrant woman masters this with grace, which should be celebrated.

Learning a new language and culture provides you with the opportunity to be a thoughtful leader as you apply your ability to think differently on your feet. Do not forget that, and make sure you use it in your success journey. Besides, knowing a second language is an advantage in our interconnected world. Furthermore, language and thought are connected, so by learning a new language, you will gain an opportunity to think differently.

3. Transformational experience: This is perhaps one of the biggest impacts of culture shock on an immigrant woman. Culture shock transforms you! To adapt to a new culture without losing your identity and original culture, you must expand your thinking, social circles, and perspectives. You have become open-minded, which opens the doors to many opportunities. The key here is to be aware and embrace the opportunities as they come. Do not shy away from them because you have already gone through the big hurdle of addressing culture shock, and you have many skills and strengths within you to succeed with confidence. Go for it! You will add a lot of richness to your life, which will bless you not only in your current state but also in your old age. Think of all the new music, food, history, and traditions you have explored. What a valuable life!

4. Love for all and appreciation for our differences: I am grateful for the opportunity to learn about other cultures, not just because of the impacts I have listed above, but also for teaching me that our differences matter. Can you imagine how boring our world would be if everything and everyone were the same? The animals, the trees, and all living creatures go about doing just what they are here to do, and all of this makes our world a much better place. Culture shock teaches us to embrace our differences because there is strength in our diversity. However, the not-so-hidden message of culture shock is that we are indeed all similar. Every human being has the same aspirations in life, regardless of how we choose to present them, i.e., we all want love. We may look for it or give it differently, but the fundamental root of everything we do is for love. *"Above all, love each other deeply because love covers over a multitude of sins."* —1 Peter 4:8 (New International Version)

Action:

• If you are currently experiencing culture shock, remind yourself that this is normal. Journal your experience as you apply some of the strategies discussed in this chapter. Life is a journey, and change is a constant, so your notes will be helpful as you journey through life. You could also share your experience with another sister on a similar journey.

• Use the TRUE technique to withstand the pressure of culture shock and your own confidence. Is this True, Right, Undeniable, and Excellent? If the thought does not meet the TRUE test, discard it quickly.

• If you have effectively adapted to your bicultural existence at this point, that is great! Be aware of this and remind yourself often of all the skills you have acquired in your journey so far. Continue to respond with openness to opportunities of cultural differences. You will come out better for these experiences. A way to remind yourself of this is by using a journal to capture your journey. Remember that I am a big fan of writing things down because it works!

Recap

Culture shock is a normal phenomenon and totally unavoidable. As you broaden your horizon, you will encounter culture shock.

The way you handle it will impact your success journey. Culture shock includes a wide range of your emotions and reactions to the sudden change in your way of life. Some examples of culture shock include food, role, language, and time.

Some of the ways you may become aware that you are experiencing culture shock include feeling extreme homesickness, hostility, anxiety, isolation, confusion, sleeping too little or too much, etc.

There are four distinct phases of culture shock. Because experiences vary from person to person, as well as in different situations, these phases sometimes feel like a cycle. The four phases are:

- **Honeymoon**
- **Crisis**
- **Adjustment**
- **Adaptation.**

The experiences of managing culture shock are transformational! You are always transitioning, and your experience will help you grow personally, be a better and well-rounded global citizen, expand your thinking, and make you appreciate differences.

Fun fact: When I think of cultural adaptation and biculturalism, I celebrate my journey by wearing bold and colorful clothing. Also, I accessorize with a red bag, shoes, earrings, and lipstick. The Bible app on my phone helps center me to who I am and who I am becoming.

In the next chapter, we continue to explore some of the challenges you may face as an immigrant woman, as well as some winning strategies to help you shine through challenging times.

CHAPTER 5

Are you Okay?

"Anything that's human is mentionable, and anything that is mentionable can be more manageable. When we can talk about our feelings, they become less overwhelming, less upsetting, and less scary."
—*Fred Rogers*

Are you okay? Like, really? Are you feeling okay?

Because of the number of women I interviewed who talked about their experiences with mental health, I was convinced I needed to write about mental health for immigrant women.

I am also aware that mental health is a subject that people don't discuss for a variety of reasons because:

- Mental health is often confused with mental illness,
- There's some stigma around mental health, especially mental illness,

- There's a lack of education and awareness around mental health, and
- Mental health, unlike physical health, is sometimes not visible.

In this chapter, I hope to shine some light on how your mental health matters in your success journey from a strength-based perspective. So, in this chapter, I would like to:

- Inform you about mental health and wellness,
- Discuss some signs that indicate that your mental health and wellness may be suffering,
- Discuss the impacts of mental health and wellness on your success journey as an immigrant woman,
- Talk about things you can do for yourself to maintain your mental health and wellness, and
- Where you can find support and help when you need it.

Mental health is for everyone

"What mental health needs is more sunlight, more candor, and more unashamed conversation." —Glenn Close

The World Health Organization defines mental health as "a state of well-being in which the individual realizes his or her own potential, can cope with the normal stresses of life, can work productively and fruitfully, and is able to make a contribution to her or his own community." (2007).

Doesn't this definition sound like success and empowerment to you?! Mental health is about how we think, feel, and act. It is a significant and necessary component to overall good health and quality of life for everyone.

Good mental health is defined not only by the absence of mental disorders and problems but also by the presence of various coping skills such as resilience, flexibility, and balance (Canadian Mental Health Association 2010). It helps us cope with life's stresses and enables us to reach our goals.

Mental health ≠ absence of mental illness

"... evidence indicates that the absence of mental illness does not imply the presence of mental health, and the absence of mental health does not imply the presence of mental illness."[14]

It's important to point out that everyone has highs and lows in their lives, and a low moment does not translate to mental illness. There may be times when you feel sad, worried, angry, or anxious due to challenges. Intermittent moments like these are normal.

Talking about mental health means talking about your mental well-being, including your emotions, thoughts, and feelings. It includes your ability to solve problems, overcome challenges and difficulties, your social connections, and your understanding of the world around you. Doesn't this sound familiar? It's exactly what we have been discussing in the strategies mentioned in all the earlier chapters. You are a holistic being, and no area of your life can be looked at without the other.

What is mental illness?

14 Keyes, C. L. (2007). Promoting and protecting mental health as flourishing: A complementary strategy for improving national mental health. American Psychologist, 62, 95-108.

Mental health is not the same as mental illness. Mental illness is when a person is diagnosed with an illness that affects how they think, feel, behave, or interact with others. Examples of mental illness include depression and anxiety disorders. When someone has a mental illness, they may require some clinical treatment, including medication as part of the overall treatment strategy. Whether or not you have a mental illness, knowing about mental health and how to keep mentally healthy is important for everyone. We can all improve our mental health.

Mental health and wellness vs. mental illness

We have established that mental health is not the same as mental illness and have looked at the different definitions. We will now look at some examples to clarify this further.

Let's imagine for a second what our health and wellness mean to us. We all know there can be no success without good health. No matter how much anyone accomplishes in life, if they have poor health, then their accomplishments are useless. Often, with some health issues, money, wealth, and success cannot buy you wholeness and peace. This is why we should all strive for good mental and physical health and wellbeing.

Your health often moves along a continuum ranging from great or good health to not-so-good health, to poor health, then to illness or disability. This is true for both physical and mental health.

Sometimes, you may have a headache or just feel unwell, but you don't necessarily have any serious illness. Likewise, people may have poor mental health without a mental illness. For instance, those days when you feel a bit down or stressed out, or even overwhelmed by someone or something that's happening in your life.

Just as it's possible to have poor mental health but no mental illness, it's also very possible to have good mental health and a diagnosis of a mental illness. Mental illnesses (like other health problems such as a broken leg) can present as episodic, meaning there are episodes of ill health and episodes of good health. In some cases, however, mental illness can be chronic.

Mental health can be gained and lost each day through our interactions and relationships. A person may not have a mental illness but can still have poor mental health. And further, a person can have a mental illness but still have good mental health.

As an immigrant woman, what you need to understand about good mental health is that it is not about feeling happy and confident 100% of the time, nor is it about ignoring all your problems. You are human, and like every other human, you will have moments of good mental health, not-so-good mental health, and poor mental health. You may also have a mental illness. What is important, though, from a good mental health and success perspective is the ability to look at problems and concerns realistically. It's about living and coping well despite problems.

With the right support and tools, anyone can live well (however they define "well") and find meaning, contribute to their communities, and work toward their goals.

A penny for your thoughts

In our lifetimes, there are many things that were once "the norm" but are no longer acceptable. This includes the voting rights of women in many cultures as well as the end of slavery. The #MeToo movement is a very recent one, arising in just the past decade. What made it easier to address these issues? It was because more and more people were talking about them. The #MeToo movement exposed the problems of sexual abuse and harrassment that many women had been suffering in silence for years, and with the momentum, it became okay to talk about and address these issues.

The point of this is that keeping silent about mental health and mental health disorders is not okay! Mental health is for everyone, and therefore, we should make an effort to talk about it more readily.

According to The Centre for Addiction and Mental Health (CAMH), in any given year:

- One in five Canadians will experience a mental illness or addiction problem[15], and
- By the time Canadians reach forty years of age, one in two have (or have had) a mental illness.

Through the lens of immigration, this data is similar for most countries. When we look at it specifically as it affects women and intersectionality, the impact on immigrant women cannot be overstated.

Immigrant women often hold multiple identities related to their immigration status, including gender, ethnicity, social class, and status. The intersections of and interplay between these dimensions of cultural identity affect not only their

15 Smetanin et al. (2011). The life and economic impact of major mental illnesses in Canada: 2011-2041. Prepared for the Mental Health Commission of Canada. Toronto: RiskAnalytica.

sociocultural experiences but also their perceptions of the world and themselves[16].

According to the Merriam-Webster Dictionary[17], intersectionality is "the complex, cumulative way in which the effects of multiple forms of discrimination (such as racism, sexism, and classism) combine, overlap, or intersect, especially in the experiences of marginalized individuals or groups."

Kimberlé Crenshaw introduced the theory of intersectionality, the idea that when it comes to thinking about how inequalities persist, categories like gender, race, and class are best understood as overlapping and mutually constitutive rather than isolated and distinct. —Adia Harvey Wingfield[18]

With the multiple issues around marginalization and the other experiences that an immigrant woman could go through, there's no doubt that she has a higher risk for numerous mental health challenges such as isolation, depression, anxiety, post-traumatic stress disorder (PTSD), psychosis, and a host of other mental health disorders.

Knowing that immigrant women are at risk of experiencing these mental health challenges, it is imperative (for us, our children and families, and the community) to start talking *and* continue to speak out about our mental health and wellness as immigrant women.

---

16 Viruell-Fuentes, E.A., P. Y. Miranda, and S. Abdulrahim. "More than Culture: Structural Racism, Intersectionality Theory, and Immigrant Health." Social Science & Medicine, vol. 75, no. 12, pp. 2099-2106
17 https://www.merriam-webster.com/dictionary/intersectionality
18 https://www.theatlantic.com/business/archive/2016/10/79-cents/504386/

Breaking the silence and stigma

"You don't have to be positive all the time. It's perfectly okay to feel sad, angry, annoyed, frustrated, scared, and anxious. Having feelings doesn't make you a negative person. It makes you human." —Lori Deschene,
Tiny Buddha: Simple Wisdom for Life's Hard Questions

So far, being silent about mental health and mental health issues has not helped anyone. What, then, is stopping us from trying the opposite? Mental health is not a simple topic, but we can find simple ways to start the conversation and build momentum as we go. We eat the elephant one bite at a time. That is how big issues are approached and addressed.

Unfortunately, many women feel too ashamed to seek help for a mental disorder. It is also disheartening that many women are simply not aware that their symptoms constitute an illness that can be treated. A big step toward improving the diagnosis and treatment of mental health conditions in women rests in education, i.e., by providing information about how common mental illness is, the importance of mental health and wellness to our overall health, the negative effects it has on women and their families, and the many resources available to help us receive the treatment we need to return to good health.

I once attended a ten-minute presentation by a gynecologist on cervical cancer. Those ten minutes have impacted my life immensely as I continue to explore ways to provide practical help to many women in the fight against cervical cancer. The gynecologist told us that it is preventable and curable. Yet, in many countries, it remains one of the top five causes of death for women. Recalling that short presentation always reminds me of the power of education and information. Another impactful education that has opened my eyes is around suicide awareness. Knowing the right things and what you can do is empowering. It can sometimes be a lifesaver: yours and many other lives as well.

Simple things we can do to break the silence and stigma around mental health include:

1. Get educated: Your health and wellness are personal. You must be the first champion of your health because many things about it depend solely on you. What do you know about mental health and mental illness? Are they myths or facts? You can find educational resources in libraries and the internet. If you do not have access to the internet or a library, you may have to get creative. If you have children and they go to school, you can send a note to their school principal or trusted teacher requesting assistance with some print resources or a connection to other relevant information, as well as service areas in your community. The hospital or your doctor's clinic is another good place to find resources. There are often handbills in different languages on many health topics, including mental health.

For many years, my knowledge of mental health was defined by what I heard growing up. It looked like a mad person. In fact, anyone experiencing a mental health or psychotic disorder was referred to as "mental". I never questioned this. I also assumed mental health disorders only happened to specific kinds of people. However, I've realized there were so many mental health problems that never got addressed because they were not even considered mental health issues in the first place.

My first immigration journey had many life changes happen around the same time, i.e., being newly married, moving away from everything that was familiar, and dealing with my first pregnancy. This triggered a lot of emotions for me. I certainly had some symptoms of poor mental health, which were unfortunately left untreated because I did not recognize them as mental health issues. I was feeling overwhelmed, lonely, I did not get a lot of sleep, I had anxiety issues because of multiple barriers with language, I struggled at doctor visits (especially because I had no clue what they were saying and I was so anxious about the baby I was carrying), and then there was the fact that no one really understood what I was going through.

My story is similar to what a lot of immigrant women experience. It is a miracle how we make it without adequate care and support. This is why knowledge is power. No one needs to go through poor mental health alone. Therefore, your success as an immigrant woman depends on knowing when you need help and making sure you get it.

2. Watch your language: Sometimes, we perpetuate the stigma around mental health and mental health disorders by the language we use and how we speak or do not speak about them. Conversations about mental health are normal, and like everything else, it should be called by its name. If someone (yourself included) is going through an episode of poor mental health, they should be shown compassion and empathy. Murmuring, laughing, and other dismissive reactions should not be entertained whether you are a bystander or the person doing it. No one sees a person who is physically hurt and then reacts in such a dismissive way. Speak up and speak out with boldness. Remember that mental health is for everyone, including you.

I facilitate suicide awareness training, and one of the things we work on in this training is using the right language to talk about suicide. When people say that a person "committed" suicide, that makes it a criminal act. This is misguided as we don't say people "committed" accidents. When people die by suicide, it is a sign that they struggled with poor mental health, and for many with thoughts of suicide, getting help and keeping safe usually avert the action itself. It is not a crime, and simply calling it suicide helps everyone get comfortable with keeping each other safe.

Since poor mental health is invisible, and the impact and reactions vary from person to person, all feelings of poor mental health and mental illness need to be taken seriously and not dismissed.

If you feel anxious, depressed, and overwhelmed, you are normal, and there is lots of support available to help you get through. Do not dismiss or diminish what you are going through or let someone else do that either. Take care of yourself by getting the necessary help you need. No one has a bad headache and dismisses it, so why dismiss anxiety attacks or depression?

3. Talk openly and honestly about mental health: This is an opportunity to choose empowerment over shame by owning your story and your life and creating the space for others to do the same. We can and must create a culture and environment where women thrive, feel confident and empowered, and are comfortable talking about their own mental health challenges (past and present) without fear of being labeled or having it affect their success. Remember, mental health is for everyone.

Just as we can freely discuss our struggles with weight gain/loss, time management, childcare and rearing, we should also be able to discuss our struggles with our mental health and wellness because everyone at some point will experience a mental health problem.

It is by naming these issues and sharing how commonly they occur that many women will get the help they need. Also, in naming them, they become more common. This is because people recognize mental health problems as something experienced by them or someone they know. Since they can relate, this helps to create normalcy instead of stigma. If I told you how overwhelmed I felt as a young mother of four children, all under six years old, and if you or a friend, a sister, or aunty had gone through a similar experience, then by sharing and talking about it, we no longer feel alone or see these things as weird.

There's no need to feel that it's "us versus them" when it comes to mental health because anyone could have a mental health issue at any point. So, do not exclude yourself from conversations on mental health, or emotional health, and wellness. Set yourself free because you are not perfect (no one is). There's no shame in being sick or feeling unwell. By sharing and speaking out, we kill the shame around mental and emotional health and wellness.

Risk factors that determine mental health status:

- Income and social status
- Education and literacy
- Employment/working conditions
- Social environments
- Physical environments
- Personal health practices and coping skills
- Healthy child development,
- Biology and genetic endowment,
- Health services,
- Gender,
- Culture, and
- Social support networks.

The list above clearly shows how broad and far-reaching mental health is. A close look at the list also shows that just about everybody could develop a mental health issue in their lifetime.

Below is another list of facts, specifically on women and mental health.

Women's mental health: Facts and figures[19]

- Women are *twice as likely* as men to be impacted by Generalized Anxiety Disorder (GAD).

19 https://online.regiscollege.edu/blog/womens-mental-health/

- The prevalence of serious mental illness is almost *70% greater* in women than in men.
- Exposure to violence makes a woman *three to four times* more likely to be affected by depression.
- Women are *twice as likely* as men to be affected by unipolar depression, which was forecast to be the second most common source of a "global disability burden" by 2020.
- Women are *more likely* to experience post-traumatic stress disorder (PTSD), and they wait much longer than men after symptoms arise to seek diagnosis and treatment.
- Women are *almost ten times more likely* than men to be affected by an eating disorder.
- Women *may be less likely* than men to seek treatment after experiencing symptoms of mental illness. This is due to "internalized or self-stigma" that results from their self-image being formed by how others perceive them.
- The stigma of seeking treatment for a mental illness *is greater among women of color.*

By now, there should be no doubt in your mind about the need as an immigrant woman to make sure you are engaged in your mental health and wellness. **But what do you do now if you are experiencing mental or emotional health issues?**

There are lots of sources of support if you have experienced a traumatic event. Aside from seeking help from trained experts such as psychologists, psychiatrists, doctors, social workers, etc., there are also things you can do to protect yourself, which include avoiding some risk factors.

Protective and risk factors

Certain factors can protect our mental health, and others can put it at risk. Those factors that protect it can help reduce the chance of developing a problem. These protective factors can also be applied when a person experiences a mental health situation. On the other hand, risk factors are those that make it more likely for a person to develop a problem. We have already discussed many of these factors and highlighted how the risks increase for many immigrant women due to immigration, discrimination, and intersectionality.

Protective and restorative factors

"One small crack does not mean that you are broken; it means that you were put to the test and you didn't fall apart." —Linda Poindexter

The key to improving mental health is to increase protective factors. Below are some factors that protect, support, and restore your mental health. As a successful immigrant woman, you must ensure that you use these strategies to effectively manage your mental and emotional health.

One Thing you can do right now to improve your mental health is to undertake mind, body, and spirit healing.

"Healing takes time and asking for help is a courageous step." —Mariska Hargitay

There are some barriers to getting good health care, and these barriers can be higher for immigrants. The barriers may include access to health care such as transportation, language, income, stigma, shame, etc. These barriers, nonetheless, should not stop you from taking care of yourself. There are lots of things you can do right now to improve your mental health. They can be looked at from the perspective of taking care of your mind, body, and spirit. Under each of the protective factors, I have shared tips and strategies to help you holistically improve the effect of your mental health on mind, body, and spirit.

I remember a low moment in my life. I felt so alone. There were people around me all the time, but I carried a heaviness, and I felt alone in my pain. My then pregnant sister had just been kidnapped, and I felt helpless, afraid, and angry. I sat and moped all day, living in a daze. There was no shine or sparkle in my heart or my eyes. Yet, I had to show up each day for my family and at work. At that time, I didn't think of my mental and emotional health. I could think of nothing other than the horror that was going on. So, with this experience, I know it is easier to suggest to someone going through a low moment that they *try* some of the tips shared in this book rather than only thinking about them.

That said, there were key things that acted as a sliver of light and brought moments of hope during my sister's twelve-day ordeal. These included:

- I prayed. I prayed hard. I had to believe that my prayer would come true. I was not just asking for my sister to be freed; I declared that she was free from the kidnappers. I saw her free in each prayer, and I felt it.
- I reached out to my church community and friends. I needed people to pray with me, and for that, it was to my church community that I went. There

were times I couldn't pray, and I knew others would continue praying for me during those moments of my weakness. The power of a supportive community cannot be overstated. My collective church groups started a global prayer chain. We had people all over the world, regardless of their language, participating in it. That was the first time I had experienced a prayer chain. I later reflected on it when friends or co-workers would share struggles they were going through, and I would flippantly say, "I'll pray for you," and do nothing. This global prayer chain gave me a new level of insight. It opened my eyes to the power of not just corporate prayers but movements, too. Think of all the movements you know, i.e., the civil rights movement, the Black Lives Matter movement, the #MeToo movement, and so many others. Do not dismiss the power of communities in your personal and collective struggles. And guess what? The friends and women from my groups fed our family all those weeks and took turns babysitting. The teachers at my kids' elementary school checked in on them (and not just their academics but also their mental health). They provided support, not only with reduced homework but, in addition, by making sure my children had buddies with them all the time, which allowed them to relax and play.

•   There was also my whole extended family. We all came together; distance was not a barrier. Everyone rallied around my brother-in-law and my young nieces, and an uncle courageously delivered the ransom, even though this was dangerous, in the hope of getting my sister back safely.

- I was alone, yes, but I did not keep quiet. I spoke up about my feelings, and that was the one thing that enabled me to function and feel energized enough to do more. This is what speaking out looks like, and it's okay. Everyone goes through stuff, some big, some small. It doesn't matter what it is because stuff is stuff, and it impacts everyone differently. So, speak out and get the support you need. It doesn't mean some things will go away, but it does mean you'll feel better, stronger, and more resilient for a richer life whatever happens.
- The other things that helped included volunteer activities and a lot of walking. Helping in the community allowed me to stop wallowing in my own thoughts. It also helped me to be grateful. Walking and moving engaged me physically and always left me feeling better. My thoughts were clearer, and I could find better ways to focus my energy on praying and sending out positive vibes to my sister.

I have summarized some of these strategies in the points below.

Protective factor #1 Strong social relationships.

Strong social relationships provide love, support, and a sense of belonging. Without any strong social network, mental health issues that may have been dormant are more likely to rear their head. Worse still, if this happens, you may not know how to deal with it because it's new and terrifying. Back in your home country, you had a great support system that worked well. Mental health issues may not have been triggered, and even when they were, they may have been well-managed, consciously or unconsciously, because of the presence of strong social networks.

Some new immigrants may not immediately have such a network when they first arrive in their host country. Ways to start building yourself a network include:

• **Tip #1– Connect with immigrant service organizations**–Immigrant and newcomer service organizations have tons of resources and information to support immigrants in navigating a host country. They also have trained experts who are familiar with immigrant experiences. These staff members can give referrals to programs and other support within the community. By connecting with organizations like them, you will meet other new immigrants and be able to cross-share information on what you are doing to help and support yourself.

• **Tip #2–Get involved in your community** – It is important (and very beneficial) to join your neighborhood communities, your home country community association, a church, or other place of worship. Participating in free programs offered through public libraries and enrolling in schools or training programs are great avenues for quickly building your social network.

• **Tip #3–Spend time with people you enjoy** – Staying connected with your family and friends, whether close by or far, can be beneficial. With technology and internet access, this is made a lot easier. However, if access to these tools is a barrier for you, there is a greater need to form new, trusted associations more quickly. When I first got to Italy, cell phones were not very common, and they had not yet arrived in Nigeria. My parents and siblings had to go to what in Nigeria were known as call centers if they wanted to take or make a phone call, and they had to visit internet cafes to access email messages. My husband connected me to some Nigerian women in the neighborhood so I could interact with people who spoke my language and understood some of my experiences. I was able to contact some of these women when I had questions.

Protective factor #2 Good physical health:

Your mental and physical health are very closely linked. The World Health Organization (WHO)[20] defines health as a state of complete physical, mental, and social well-being and not merely the absence of disease or infirmity. The WHO states: "There is no health without mental health."[21] Sometimes, when I am anxious, emotionally troubled, or overwhelmed, I get headaches and cold-like symptoms such as aches and pains in many parts of my body. Does this happen to you? There's no doubt about the connection between our physical health and our mental health. Being aware of the link between mind and body is the first step in developing strategies to reduce the incidence of co-existing mental and chronic physical health conditions. It's also very important to be aware that the relationship between mental and physical health is most

20 https://www.who.int/about/who-we-are/frequently-asked-questions
21 Promoting mental health: concepts, emerging evidence, practice: summary report / a report from the World Health Organization, Department of Mental Health and Substance Abuse in collaboration with the Victorian Health Promotion Foundation (VicHealth) and the University of Melbourne. (2004).

pronounced with chronic conditions like diabetes, cancer, high blood pressure, etc.

Poor mental health has a direct impact on your immune system and is a risk factor for chronic physical conditions. Likewise, having a chronic physical condition increases the risk of developing poor mental health. Therefore, maintaining or improving our physical health benefits overall health. Here are some tips on improving and maintaining your physical and mental health in turn:

- **Tip #1–Exercise:** Daily physical activity benefits your health. There are many ways to incorporate movement into your daily life and routine. You do not need a gym membership. You can take walks, or you can use a jump rope, dance, go for a bike ride, jog, swim, etc. Stick to activities you enjoy for at least thirty minutes a day, so they are effortless yet impactful.

- **Tip #2 –Get enough sleep:** Rest is a weapon! In the scriptures, there are many instances of Jesus going away to a quiet place to rest. In the story of creation, we are also told that God rested on the seventh day. Don't you feel refreshed and rejuvenated after a good rest? I know I do. Yet, I sometimes do not prioritize it. Why is it so easy to forget so quickly how good it feels to take a rest, especially a much needed one?

    Sleep is fundamental to a healthy mind and body and getting a good night's sleep can make a huge difference in your overall health. It plays a role in your moods, your ability to learn and make memories, the health of your organs, how well your immune system works, and other bodily functions like appetite, metabolism, and hormone release. This is why it feels so good when you wake up after a good sleep. You function so much better and can avoid mental health issues.

Prioritize sleep to protect your mental health. While needs can vary depending on your age, aim to get more than six hours of sleep each night. Some things that may help include following a regular routine, reducing and/or avoiding caffeine and alcohol, winding down with a good book or bath, and keeping your room dark, cool, and electronic-free.

- **Tip #3–Watch what you eat and drink:** The quality of the food you eat can impact your overall physical and mental health. Eating nutritious foods in moderation like fruits, vegetables, beans, rice, meat, fish, grains, and most natural foods can go a long way toward achieving a healthy lifestyle. In many countries, fast food is cheap, convenient, and offered in large quantities; however, it may cause more damage than good over the long haul, and medical issues could be more expensive than all the money you may have saved by living off it.

It is a myth that nutritious food is expensive. Even on a budget, there are many ways to prepare tasty, nutritious meals for yourself and your family. With my family of six, I always buy fruits that are in season, frozen fruits and vegetables, eggs, beans, lentils, and canned fish, as well as discounted fresh produce that I can blanch or cook and freeze. I also cook in bulk and remake leftovers.

Research shows that diet is linked to the hippocampus, the area of the brain involved in learning, memory, and mental health. It is said that people with healthy diets have more hippocampal volume than those with unhealthy ones. Making changes to your diet can take some planning, but it is worth your while. If you are struggling in making this change, try participating in cooking co-ops with others. You will feel so much better if most of your meals are nutritious and tasty.

Additionally, do not forget to drink water to quench your thirst. Keep hydrated for blood circulation, smooth skin, and so many other positives. Look at what water does to plants and other living creatures for a good visual of what it could also do for you as a living organism!

Protective factor #3 Feeling in control of your life and bouncing back when life happens:

All people have many emotions, and women even more so. Positive emotions support our mental health. Have you ever noticed how much better you manage and respond to stress when you experience emotions like peace, joy, security, stability, abundance, love, happiness, etc.? The ability to manage and express our emotions well can improve our overall health. I will admit that it's not always easy to have a positive outlook, especially when dealing with transitions and traumatic life events. And that's okay. It's okay to feel what you feel at that moment. It's okay to take your time and process it all later, then when you can, **start healing**. Resilience helps us in that process of healing and restoration. It allows us to bounce back positively from hard times and helps us focus on the things we can control to protect our mental and emotional health. These qualities equip us to plan, problem-solve, and develop healthy coping strategies when "life happens".

Every time you make it through life's challenges, you strengthen your ability and capacity to handle future stressors. Isn't it empowering to know that you grow as a result of these pains?

Below are some practical tips to help you in being resilient and positive in life.

- **Tip #1–Find your anchor:**
We are all spiritual beings.

"We are not human beings having a spiritual experience. We are spiritual beings having a human experience."
—*Pierre Teilhard de Chardin.*

This is not about religion or some other beliefs. It is a fact that most people on this earthly journey recognize there's a higher power out there. We are not just mind and body. We are mind, body, *and* spirit. By anchoring onto a higher power, no matter how fierce the storm is or how hard the wind blows, you will always bounce back. It's only a matter of time. If, however, you do not have a solid anchor in something higher than you are, you will struggle.

So, what does anchoring onto a higher power look like? Think of an actual anchor that is used by sailors. It gets firmly planted into the bottom of the ocean floor and provides the ship with the stability it needs while also keeping the people aboard the ship safe. Therefore, the anchor is a symbol of stability, hope, and steadfastness.

"One who has control over the mind is tranquil in heat and cold, in pleasure and pain, and in honor and dishonor." —Bhagavad Gita.

Anchoring onto a higher power gives you hope and stability because you know that something higher than you is at play and in control. This might look like being out in nature, helping other people in need, meditating, or praying.

- **Tip #2–Do what you enjoy and find your purpose:** What moves you? Music, sports, reading, dancing, painting, drawing, etc.? The point is, whatever gives you peace and good energy relieves stress. Also, finding purpose and meaning in life promotes positive mental health. It can be a source of strength and inspiration or a means of coping with life and aiding personal growth. This may include spiritual beliefs, religious practices, worship, and/or other activities that have meaning. Take time to review what matters to you and find ways to celebrate life. Conversely, do not get sucked into things that take your energy away from you. Engage in activities and relationships that boost your positive energy, not those that drain them. You need a lot of energy to confidently and successfully navigate your life journey.

- **Tip #3–Get involved in your community:** Have you explored art and cultural events and festivals in your community? Do you know about community gardens and yoga classes in your neighborhood? Getting involved in your community is a good way to feel useful. There are many benefits to taking part in local programs and projects. You get a chance to create new things and connect with others. You will also share your talents with your community and know what's going on around you. You have more exposure to the culture as you make new friends. Opportunities to volunteer and assist others also help you to increase feelings of good mental well-being. By getting involved, you will build strong relationships (and we already discussed the value of strong social networks on your overall health and wellness).

Action:

Are you okay? Just stop and answer this question honestly. If you feel overwhelmed, stressed, burned out, heavy, anxious, depressed, lonely, or emotionally and mentally unwell, stop whatever you are doing right now. Yes, that means stop reading right now and take three deep breaths. As you breathe in, tell yourself you are breathing in health and wellness. As you breathe out, tell yourself you are loosening whatever you are feeling: loneliness, sadness, anxiety, depression, etc. If you are feeling great, do the exercise anyway, as it will help you refocus better on whatever you are doing at that moment. You can breathe in gratitude, confidence, and power and release love as you breathe out.

Now that you have released some of your negative emotions by taking three breaths in and out, grab your journal, and create a mental health coping strategy for yourself. You can call it your energy station, like a gas station where you fill up your energy tank. Make a list of the top five things that fill your energy tank and the five top things that drain it. Then, whenever you feel low, make sure to fill up your tank with one or more of the energy fillers and do less of or eliminate one or more of the energy drainers. For example, listening to gospel music and praising God fills my tank all the time. On the other hand, spending too much time on WhatsApp drains my energy, so either I "fast" from it for a certain period, or I spend a very minimal amount of time on it, or I only use it when communicating with specific people.

Make a resource list of where to go for help or who to connect with when you need support.

Recap

Mental health is for everyone. You must take care of it, and to do so, it is beneficial to learn the facts and talk about mental health.

Promoting mental health to **everyone**, including you as an immigrant woman:

- Improves mental health,
- Reduces stigma, and
- Helps people to recognize the risks and get help.

There is evidence that women have it rougher than men when it comes to mental health. This is even worse for immigrant women due to having multiple risk factors present in their lives. The biggest barriers that you face with mental health and mental illness are stigma and shame. Talking freely about mental health and educating yourself on mental health are two simple ways to eliminate this stigma.

Building strong social networks, maintaining good physical health, and being resilient are some factors that protect, support, and restore your mental health.

If you have concerns about yourself or someone you care about, talk with a professional because the tips in this book are not a substitute for professional assistance.

For immediate help, call 911 (or whatever happens to be the emergency line where you live) or visit your nearest hospital emergency department.

Fun fact: I always carry a rosary in my bag. Meditating with the rosary is peaceful and helps me to re-center. What can you easily reach for that helps you to be mindful?

CHAPTER 6

Jumping Hurdles

"Going to a country where you don't speak the language is like wading into the sea when you can't swim—it's intimidating at first, not impossible, and ultimately manageable." —Stewart Stafford

In this chapter, I highlight two common challenges faced by immigrants and explore how these experiences build your confidence and enlighten your immigration story.

Language barriers are the biggest challenge most immigrants face, followed closely by attaining desired employment. These challenges can prevent an immigrant woman from reaching her full potential. Take the following experience as an example:

"What is your name?" they asked in Italian.

As I had no clue what they were saying, I smiled sheepishly and heard my husband say, "Anne," before spelling out my name. And everyone repeated: "Ann-e." So he said "Anna," and they all nodded and smiled. And that became my new name for the time I lived in Italy. The Italians pronounce every letter, and even though the "e" in my middle name is silent, they would still say it.

My husband had explained to me that going by "Ify" would be even more challenging and quite an experience; he had navigated this same issue and went by his middle name because his Igbo name was difficult for many people to pronounce.

However, the good news is that there are ways to break down these kinds of barriers and harness the experience to your advantage by leveraging the skill of scenario planning. It makes you address the question: **If** I can communicate in different ways, **then**... I can confidently navigate relationships and have a voice (or whatever words you choose to fill in the blank).

Language barriers

While we are talking about names, it's important to point out that this is one of the first language barriers many immigrants face. Not only does a name highlight the existence of language barriers, but it also plays a key factor in a job search. Also, my name is a big part of my identity. It tells others where I am from, but it's also a lot more than that. When I was literally forced to adopt a new name ("Anna"), I had to learn to recognize that it was my name. And I assure you, answering to an unplanned new name in my adult years was not an easy task. It demanded a lot of mental energy.

So it is with learning a new language. It requires a heck of a lot of mental energy. When immigrating, you may have to learn to understand and speak a new language to survive, and that alone is stressful. On top of that stress, your brain is constantly working on translating. It is going back and forth from your first language to the new language with every single word you hear or want to speak.

The impact a language barrier has on an immigrant's confidence and mental/emotional wellbeing cannot be appropriately expressed in full. Even when you live this experience, you can't quite put it in words. I had to observe this event in the lives of others to understand the full impact it has on immigrants. When I was a newcomer in Italy and knew zero Italian, I felt helpless, lost, afraid, and angry. I am an introvert but finding myself in this situation made me even more silent, and it took several months for me to realize the impact this had on my risk factors.

The moment of this realization is always fresh in my mind. It was a few months after I'd had my first baby, and I was getting ready to go to church. I wasn't aware that I was singing out loud, and I suddenly stopped when I realized my husband was watching me. He simply said, "That's the first time I've heard you sing since you came to Italy." His comment caused me to realize that for more than a year, I had apparently never sung aloud, even though I used to sing in the church choir. I had been unaware that I was slowly losing "my voice".

Several years later, in Canada, when I found myself in a classroom setting amid other immigrants, I had a visceral recollection of the emotions and stress I had gone through concerning the language barrier. My classmates were internationally trained professionals who struggled to integrate and express themselves in another language. Their frustrations were intense. Unfortunately, many in the group were not successful due to setbacks with the language. Many of them became successful in other things, but this experience was an initial blow to their confidence and self-esteem.

The need to understand what people are saying and to be understood is very basic. When you learn the language of a host country, a new workplace, or a new educational program, you not only fit in, but you also do well. Language is one of the central factors that influences how fast you become acculturated. Learning the language of the host country also helps you develop self-esteem and a sense of mastery.

When immigrant women are conversant and articulate well, they are in a better position to explore aspects of their abilities, interests, and identity. They can also self-advocate, use their "voice", and accumulate resources to help them on their journey.

The power of language

"Language is power, in ways more literal than most people think. When we speak, we exercise the power of language to transform reality. Why don't more of us realize the connection between language and power?" —Julia Penelope

A lot of women remain silent, marginalized, discontented, victimized, excluded, and disengaged in social and personal interactions because of language barriers. There's a lot of power imbalance caused by these barriers. A lack of language proficiency also causes some immigrant women to be perceived as social misfits and intellectually inferior.

Can you see how much power language wields? It has such an enormous influence on our everyday lives. We must be able to name and discuss things accurately in order to solve problems.

Deficiency labeling

One of the problems with language barriers is its deficient label. The word "barrier" is quite negative. Unfortunately, with this labeling, when someone is yet to master a new language, it imposes a weakness not just on the skill (i.e., the language itself) but on the whole person. If I lack a particular competence (including a core competence like language), it does not diminish who I am. I can and will learn the skill if I need to, and while learning, it does not diminish other things I bring to the table. Knowing this can boost your confidence as you navigate the language experience. Do not allow yourself to be beaten down by others or yourself. You have learned and mastered many skills in your lifetime, and this will be no different.

Negotiating language barriers

"Everyone smiles in the same language." —George Carlin

As an immigrant, even when you speak in the same language used in the host country, you will run into challenges while communicating. When that happens, remember that everyone you speak to is human, too. Responses to your communication struggles may differ from person to person; however, most people are understanding, helpful, and appreciative of your effort. So, don't be discouraged, even though it is frustrating when you are struggling to be understood, or in turn, to understand others.

Language barriers can be tackled in different ways. Education, both formal and informal, is the best way to get up to speed. Aside from learning the new language by using apps like *Duolingo* and enrolling in a local beginner's language course, here are a few other things you can do as you navigate and negotiate this challenge:

- **Peer circles:** The peer circle system is where you collaborate with other women and keep each other accountable for progress. It is a great strategy in negotiating language barriers. You can make it fun by cross-learning each other's languages through friendly conversation circles. This will also improve your relationships. Peer circles can provide a safe space to talk about your struggles and/or learn from those encountered by other women when adapting to change.

- **Code switch:** Code-switching between languages is a great tool, and it naturally happens when one has been exposed to different cultures. It stems out of the need to be socially accepted. Some people may have a problem with code-switching; however, we are often told in public speaking, as well as in writing, to remember our audience. For me, code-switching is exactly that. According to Dictionary.com, code-switching means "the modifying of one's speech, behavior, appearance, etc. to adapt to different sociocultural norms."[22] As such, everyone that speaks more than one language does this even if they don't call it code-switching. When my kids were toddlers, they knew to tell any black "uncle or aunty" who asked for their names, their Igbo names, regardless of whether the "uncle or aunty" was Igbo or not. And they instinctively did this without any help or tutoring by my husband or

---

22 https://www.dictionary.com/e/code-switching/

me. Likewise, when a white person asked them their names, they would not provide their Igbo names. They told them their Italian names instead. It just happened naturally. Don't be shy or apologetic if you code-switch. Remember that a person who knows more than one language can do this, and it's natural. However, do not use code-switching to mask our authentic self.

- **Discomfort:** Immersing yourself in common places where you will be forced to use the language is another strategy you could use. This might be uncomfortable at first, but I promise you that after a few mistakes, you will get better at it. Pushing yourself outside your comfort zone is where growth happens. At first, being okay and not worrying about grammar is most important. As you get used to hearing yourself speak, be corrected by others, and laugh at yourself a lot, you will find that you improve daily. Using public transit or taxis can force you to communicate, especially if you are not just shoving the address in the driver's face. If you are the outgoing type, you may also try restaurants where many locals go for lunch. You are sure to strike up a conversation in these kinds of places. Putting yourself out there can be matched with watching (listening to) TV shows. This was one of the fastest ways I learned Italian. I watched a lot of children's cartoons and learned quickly. I found out that children's shows tend to be repeated very frequently and as we all know, repeatedly doing something leads to mastery.

We might all agree by now that language is a big concern and challenge for immigrant women, so we will go straight to breaking this barrier, and better still, turning the experience into a success strategy.

Have you listened to Brené Brown, the queen of vulnerability? If not, I would recommend you look up her Ted Talk on the subject of vulnerability. I love what Brené says about shame, and this can be applied to how vulnerable a language barrier makes immigrants and newcomers feel.

Tips for flipping a language barrier into an opening for success:

"Migrants have crossed many barriers in search of a better life, crossing the language barrier is something we can do to clear the path to justice."[23] —*Claire Morris*

- **Reframe your thinking:** Brené Brown, in her book *Daring Greatly,* talks about grappling with intimidating situations as being acts of courage rather than weakness. Navigating cultural and language differences is intimidating. By venturing outside your comfort zone and embracing feelings of discomfort, you are being courageous, and this is nothing to be ashamed of. Being courageous is a respectable act. So, embrace the fact that you are learning a new language and don't let your baby steps, your mistakes, and your falls hold you back. Consider it a strength that you are one of the few people who speak a second or third language. If you master this act of successfully reframing with

23 https://wearerestless.org/2020/10/02/how-language-barriers-amplify-power-imbalances-in-migrant-camps/

learning new ways of communicating, you will go a long way in your success journey. This is something you can apply to any challenge or intimidating circumstance. Besides, if you overcome a huge test such as mastering a new language, you can definitely overcome other things.

•   **Use other common languages generously:** Before I could speak Italian, I had to come up with alternative ways to communicate. Spoken language is only seven percent of overall communication techniques; the rest of the ninety-three percent is non-verbal. While non-verbal is usually referred to as tone of voice and body language, I discovered that using images was also powerful. Since I could not use written words with my limited Italian, sketching became a powerful tool of expression for me. I was not the best of artists, but this was not important. People usually made out what I was sketching and would often sketch back their responses. So I learned always to have a tiny notebook and a pen in my handbag wherever I went. I also started writing some common words in my notebook and would use them in combination with my pocket dictionary to communicate wherever I went. To this day, whether at work or with my children, pictures are tools that always help us to clarify and understand each other better. Besides, I loved word problems in math, so when there's an issue, I reframe it as if I am dealing with a word problem in elementary school and solve it by presenting it visually. Notice how I use the two strategies of reframing and sketching to communicate and solve problems? You, too, can find similar ways to apply what you have learned from experiencing language challenges in other situations. And even by using non-verbal actions more generously, you will discover the wealth of language you have in common with others.

• **Hone your interpersonal skills:** Learning a new language affords immigrant women a great opportunity! Consciously or subconsciously, any smart immigrant woman who wants to communicate despite the language barrier will find ways to use other skills to survive. As you know, when a person has a disability, say a blind person, they compensate with heightened use of their other senses like touch, hearing, and smell. That you must communicate, regardless of whether you know the language, likewise opens up opportunities for you to combine skills that aren't usually used in communication. Some of the strategies I use include:

◇ I write down what I want to ask. This enables me to ask richer questions.

◇ I naturally ask questions, and more so when there are communication challenges. This helps me to clarify what is being talked about and helps others to be clearer in their communications as well.

◇ I summarize my points. Sometimes, to confirm I have the right details, I may slowly repeat what I have written. Other times, I just do this for my own benefit because as I write, it helps me process the conversation while challenging me to think critically. After being a stay-at-home mom for almost ten years, the first corporate job I got was because the hiring manager was impressed by my notetaking. She thought it showed a lot of interest in the role, and it also indicated that I already knew what was needed for the job.

You got this!

"The world is a book, and those who do not travel read only a page." —Augustine of Hippo

There's no escaping the struggles with language and communication in a new setting. And that is okay! You will find your pace as you navigate this huge challenge. As you go, know that these three things are certain:

1. Language barriers will cause you some problems.
2. You will find a way.
3. You will eventually be able to look back, laugh at yourself, and appreciate the wealth of communication skills you have developed.

Remember that by taking the leap to live in a new country with a new language, you have made the choice to take yourself out of your comfort zone. Facing challenges allows you to grow and become a more confident, enlightened, and successful woman. So, be proud of yourself and get on with knocking down those barriers!

The world of work

"Let the favor of the Lord our God be upon us and establish the work of our hands upon us; yes, establish the work of our hands!" —Psalm 90:17 (English Standard Version).

In the previous sections of part two, we explored some challenges and discussed ways to leverage the learning opportunities they provide. By making lemonade from these "lemons", personal transformation happens. For many immigrant women, finding meaningful employment is not initially easy and may be discouraging. Yet, we can find ways to make more lemonade (and money) from the challenges of finding the employment we not only desire but are also skilled to do.

This part of chapter six takes a look at some of the hard-core facts that immigrants may face. In our usual fashion, we "make lemonade out of the lemons" because we can turn these challenging experiences into empowering skills for our everyday success.

The workplace

Employment is recognized worldwide as an important social determinant of health (the World Health Organization, 2008). Work provides income and self-identification, whereas the lack of work correlates directly with poor health. The absence of employment creates isolation, marginalization, material and financial deprivation, and erodes one's self-confidence. As identified in the chapter above on your mental and emotional health, a lack of employment is a risk factor to your mental health. On the other hand, **meaningful work** fosters mental well-being because it is a source of social networking, social support, and self-esteem. It is a major contributor to social status, economic independence, and recognition from others.

Meaningful work: at different times in my life journey, I have been a stay-at-home mom as well as a woman working outside the home. My definition of meaningful work is work that makes a difference, impacting both society and **me** positively. So, I will be one of the first to point out that the definition of work as society sees it already marginalizes women. Some of the work that women do in the home (especially as full-time, stay-at-home moms) is often not seen as work because the pay may not translate into physical cash. But this *is* meaningful work. When a woman stays home, if quantified monetarily, the time, energy, talent, and skills she expends in doing all the work she gets done in the number of hours she does would show our governments and household units the billions of dollars being generated by these women.

Just imagine all the shopping, cooking, cleaning, and caring for babies and the elderly that goes on, unpaid, and which is mostly done by women! If all these tasks were contracted out to these same women, they would be running Instacart businesses, restaurants, janitorial services, daycare and senior care centers, which would create a lot of tax dollars and family incomes!

For any immigrant woman in the season of doing meaningful work inside the home, you are not left out in this conversation, for sure. Take what applies to you in this moment and use the rest of the strategies described below when the timing works better for you.

If we go back to some of the challenges presented by a lack of employment to an immigrant woman looking to work outside the home, the risks to her mental health double when all the other challenges unique to immigrants are considered.

According to a Statistics Canada labor market report[24], unfortunately for new immigrants in Canada, findings reveal that between two and four years after arrival, 54% are still looking for meaningful work.

Common employment barriers

The reality is that in the current economic times, finding meaningful employment is challenging for everyone, including recent graduates from our colleges and universities. Below are some of the unique struggles that an immigrant woman may experience while looking for such employment:

- **De-skilling:** Unfortunately, foreign credentials are devalued in some host countries, which places immigrants in situations that expose them to discriminatory work practices and pay and gender inequality. De-skilling is defined as the system in which foreign education and credentials are not recognized by the host country (Bauder, 2003, p. 701).
  - ◊ Rigorous certification systems in some host countries often favor individuals who have that country's education, training, and work experience. Immigrants then become discriminated against based on where they got their education and training.

Some recommendations to bridge the gap presented by de-skilling are:

- Check the credential evaluation and assessment process for your training. This will limit the

24 https://www.canada.ca/en/immigration-refugees-citizenship/corporate/reports-statistics/research/initial-labour-market-outcomes-comprehensive-look-employment-experience-recent-immigrants-first-four-years-canada.html accesed March 3, 2021

re-skilling and upskilling you may need to do to get back on track.

• Connect with professional organizations to keep abreast of programs. They may fast-track or provide other ways for you to move forward in your area of expertise. They may also offer networking opportunities, which are an important resource for finding meaningful employment.

• Invest in education and training. This works for everyone regardless of their level of education. Education was named by all the women I interviewed as the one thing that led to their success and integration into their host country workforces. Education and training include professional training as well as enrolling in programs focused on readjustment, and we will discuss the topic further in the next section.

Discrimination: In recent times, the number of women who immigrate with higher levels of education is on the rise. Yet you will find low numbers of skilled female workers (with only the minority in upper segments of the workforce). On the other hand, you will find more immigrant women in low-wage, low-skill service sectors. It does appear that the labor market system in some of these countries, where foreign education and training are not regarded, discriminates against women with those credentials.

Most hiring processes favor education, training, and work experience from the host country. While discrimination is often systemic, it impacts your mental health, and this makes it imperative that you find ways to support your health and wellbeing.

You must know who you are and have the self-confidence to know you are worth more than your current situation. Power on; get that education and show your worth as you contribute meaningfully to society. However, this is easier said than done, and applying some of the tips we've already discussed in the previous chapters on clarity, identity, transition planning, acculturation, and mental health and wellness will help to lift you up and push you forward in your success journey.

Language barriers: As we discussed earlier in this chapter, this is a major challenge that immigrants face. It adds to the employment problem as communication is the bedrock of any social environment, including workplaces. Immigrant women with higher language proficiency tend to be employed in higher-skilled jobs. The tips discussed earlier in the language section will help in combating this roadblock on your success journey. Education, once again, will come to your rescue in dealing with this challenge.

The way forward

"We need women who are so strong they can be gentle, so educated they can be humble, so fierce they can be compassionate, so passionate they can be rational, and so disciplined they can be free." —Kavita Ramdas

As an immigrant woman, though you may experience some of the barriers mentioned (i.e., difficulties in foreign credential recognition, adaptation to a different cultural environment and language, dismissal of education and experience obtained abroad, increased experiences of discrimination, and significantly lower initial earnings), you will overcome! Having come this far, there's nothing that can hold you back. Many going before you have scaled these barriers and overcome them.

Below are proven tools (or items for your handbag) that work in whatever stage of your success journey you are. It doesn't matter if you are just setting out as a fresh newcomer or have been in the country for many years.

Job-ready: What's in her handbag

• **Job search skills:** Work on your job search skills, including resumé writing, marketing (your selling points, i.e., your international experiences), interview preparation, and professional networking. These skills will assist you with an easier transition into the work environment and will also increase your knowledge of working life in your new country. They will also bring you up to speed with the laws and the rights and responsibilities of both employers and employees.

◊ Resources for newcomers in obtaining job search skills and connections include immigrant service organizations, professional organizations, public libraries, mentors, and career coaches. If you already have a resumé or CV, it pays to use these resources to determine what is acceptable in the workplace of your current environment. These organizations will help you understand how employers hire and the skills they value.

◊ If you have been in the country for a while (whether looking for work for the first time or interested in making a change), working with a career coach is beneficial. One of the tools I effectively used when I was ready to rejoin the workforce after being a stay-at-home mom for ten years was **informational interviews**. I identified women working corporate jobs, wrote out five questions (there are many good sample questions online), and emailed them asking for twenty-to-thirty minutes of their time. Though requesting informational interviews is uncomfortable, remember that we grow when we are outside of our comfort zone. Besides, most people like to talk about themselves, are good people at heart, and like to help others. Here's my tip on getting the names of people to interview:

» Start with someone you know.

» Once you've interviewed her, ask her to refer you to two or three other women you could talk to as well.

» Send a follow-up thank you and ask nicely again for ideas and other successful women to interview.

• **Soft skills:** What makes you get along with people? Most times, it's not just because of what you know but more about how you relate to people. I call this "people skills" or "soft skills". According to Dictionary.com, soft skills are "personal attributes that enable someone to interact effectively and harmoniously with other people." As already pointed out, most immigrant women with foreign credentials would need to retrain or pivot into another field. However, that is not the only hurdle. Even with technical skills under your belt, you need good interpersonal skills to be successful in the workplace.

This is because, in some instances, working on your interpersonal skills will grant you quicker access than technical skills. You can learn soft skills by taking on transitional jobs and by volunteering. Make sure you document these experiences so you can update your portfolio as you move ahead.

I was fortunate to attend a four-month work integration program shortly after we arrived in Canada. Though I also attended a host of other programs, I felt this program was most beneficial because it provided the relevant skills for integrating quickly into the Canadian workplace. The key soft skills I got from the training, which I would recommend for your success, include:

◇ Knowledge of the Canadian workplace, its labor context, and business culture.

◇ Knowledge of job search skills and the proper preparation of documents.

◇ Increase in self-confidence and self-esteem.

◇ Robust knowledge of community resources.

◇ An opportunity to build a social network with other immigrant women as we shared our stories, struggles, and strategies.

• **Network power:** You must have heard this common saying: "It's not about what you know, but who you know." I think this is universal. Personal referrals work for many things, including finding employment. Being new in a place means your network is pretty much non-existent, and with all the other work you have to do, networking is very important. It is one of those tricky things that many of us (myself included) really don't like to involve ourselves in. When you talk about embracing discomfort, networking ranks high. This is because we fear rejection. We don't know how others will perceive us when we reach out to people we don't know. Networking is awkward for most people. However, no matter how awkward it is, it does work and is a great tool to use to grow your social circles, become informed, and be employed through the hidden job market. Like informational interviews, preparing before a networking event helps. Some tips to help with networking are:

◇ Do some preparatory work and know what the event is about, including the kind of people you may meet. Is it a professional gathering or a social function with people of mixed backgrounds? I often treat any gathering as a networking practice opportunity, be it at church, a party, a funeral, or outside the school while parents waited for their kids to come out. This way, when I am at a formal networking event, I pretend it's just like my practice sessions.

◇ If possible, go with someone you know. You can initially hang out with this person when you first arrive so you can familiarize yourself with your surroundings. Just make sure you do not hang out with that person for the whole event, as this would defeat the purpose of the networking opportunity.

◇ Wear something you are comfortable in. This will be one less thing to worry about. Your state of dress not only creates a good first impression but also helps boost your self-confidence.

◇ Relax, and don't make the event about what you want. Be prepared to pitch yourself or share a business card/resumé but remember that engaging with people to get to know them better will build a longer-lasting impression, which is ultimately more fruitful in building relationships.

• **Career goals:** It is important to know where you are headed. It may take some time to get there; however, as we already explored in the clarity chapter above, not having a clear idea of your destination may take you very far from your dream. Therefore, it is important to set your career goals as this will help you identify opportunities when they present themselves. Some of these may come in the form of training, education, or volunteering. Without goals, you may not see these opportunities as such. For example, I knew I wanted to continue working on getting my professional qualification in Canada. I also did not want to spend years doing this since I already had prior education before spending many years as a stay-at-home mom. This helped me ask questions that were different but important to my goals and led me to discover a program targeting internationally trained accountants by helping them challenge entrance exams[25] for professional training. If I had not boldly asked specific questions and had simply trusted that I could sit back and wait for an opportunity to become available, I might eventually have gotten to my destination. However, it would

25 https://www.cpacanada.ca/-/media/site/operational/ec-education-certification/docs/g10487-ec_challenge-exam-policy-faqs_en.pdf accessed on May 3, 2021

have been a long and expensive route. The point is, if you set career goals that are specific, you will be pulled toward achieving those goals.

- **Entrepreneurship:** Many immigrants choose to set up their own businesses. This is a great option, especially with freelancing these days, which does not require a lot of capital to set up. There are many resources to help women who want to run their own shows. Still, you will need to do some initial training and educate yourself—not just about your specific business but in successfully running one. Do not neglect this option, as many immigrant women do well and flourish as business owners. If it speaks to you, explore it and see where it leads. You can also start small while you flesh out the opportunity.

Rejection: The art of turning lemons into lemonade

I'd sent in my application, and I was excited when I was called in for an interview. I prepared very well and was very ready. I went to the interview and then waited to be offered the job. And then I waited some more. When I followed up after a few weeks, I was told someone else had been offered the position. The cycle repeated, and I began to think the problem was me.

With all the items we've discussed above already in your handbag, you are well on your way to entering the world of work. But it's not entirely smooth sailing. There's no denying the fact that you will suffer some form of rejection at least once. Rejection hurts, but it is a great teacher, too. I guess you may already have realized that we would be learning from this pain, especially because we all experience rejection in one form or the other at some point on our journey. Therefore, it's important to have some tools in our handbags to be able to deal with rejection and still come out successful on the other end.

Rejection is a common problem faced by many immigrants hoping to get back to their profession, at least to where they left off in their home country. Here I will share some strategies to help you prepare for rejection and turn it into opportunities for success. Your journey should not be derailed by these experiences, which though they will hurt, are not insurmountable.

Do you remember the program I mentioned for internationally trained accountants that I was fortunate to be a part of? Well, I almost didn't make the list. I was initially rejected because my English assessment score was too high. One of the criteria was that the newcomer had to have a lower than average proficiency with the English language.

When I first received this feedback, I was sad, then annoyed, and I wondered why I hadn't been told in time to flunk the language assessment. My heart felt heavy; I hadn't imagined that someone could be disqualified for being proficient at something. Then I remembered a lesson from the scriptures, namely The Parable of the Persistent Widow (Luke 18:1–8). A judge who lacks compassion is repeatedly approached by a poor widow seeking justice.

So, instead of giving up, I made a case for myself, describing the benefits of giving people like me an opportunity. I was persistent and asked about other options that might be available. The program coordinator finally decided to present my case to the funders, and luckily, they agreed to waive that criterion. I know that not all rejection ends this way, but I hope this encourages you not to give up on yourself in any situation you are in.

The potion for the sting

Rejection hurts. I mean, it stings. No one likes rejection. Big rejection, like not getting that job or grant for the project, or small rejection, like not getting many views and likes on social media, is something we all experience many times. In fact, research has shown that the same parts of the brain that light up when we experience physical pain also light up when we experience rejection. Studies have shown that some people who were given Tylenol after rejection (just as they would normally take if they fell and hurt their backs) reported that the hurt and pain of the rejection subsided.

It's not about whether we experience rejection; it is about when we experience it what we do to ensure it does not derail our journey. How do you resist the fear of rejection and still make sure you are putting yourself out there? We grow when we embrace the uncomfortable.

"Whenever you feel uncomfortable, instead of retreating back into your old comfort zone, pat yourself on the back and say, 'I must be growing', and continue moving forward." —T. Harv Eker, Secrets of the Millionaire Mind

Failure and rejection

When you fail at something, it is usually a specific task you didn't do well. With rejection, it's much more. It's different. Rejection is tied to social acceptance, so it hurts more. And for an immigrant woman who may already be battling with acceptance and integration into a new society, the pain of rejection is like pouring salt into an open wound.

You may be wondering, what good can come from this experience? If you burn your fingers on a hot stove, your brain knows not to do that ever again. Does this mean that if you are rejected, you should never again step out of your comfort zone? No. It should tell you that you may need to do things differently. Though you will not be able to override the pain, you heal faster if you are aware of the issue and call rejection what it is. This helps you focus on what you have control over. Thus, knowing that this pain or reaction is not unique to you is a good first step.

Steps to handling rejection:

- **Revive your self-esteem:** Being rejected does not mean you are bad or have no good qualities. You need to remember that it is not a life and death matter, but rather that there are things you are good at that will be of benefit elsewhere. Take a moment to write out your positive attributes and brainstorm other ways that they will serve others. If you keep a gratitude journal, this is a good time to list at least three things about you that are awesome!
- **Let it go:** Our response to rejection is automatic, just like physical pain. Before you start wallowing in that pain, take some time to ask yourself if this specific experience is really of consequence. Then ask yourself if you should spend your time dwelling on that ill feeling. Was this a rejection by someone who matters, like family or a trusted friend? Mostly, we spend time on things and people that do not really matter to us. Wasting your energy and time on irrelevant and inconsequential things will keep you

back from making progress. Let it go and continue your journey by focusing on what is important.

- **It's not really about you:** Yes, it happened to you, but most times, rejection is not personal. It's neither because of something you have done or not done nor is it something you don't have. It is often situational. For example, you didn't get the job because they don't know you well. You didn't get the contract, not because of your abilities but because they did not understand your abilities fully at the interview. Do not internalize the rejection as something that was strictly about you. It happened to you, but *it is not you.*
- **The benefit of the doubt:** I always give others and myself the benefit of the doubt. This, of course, is not easy. My take is that human beings are complicated—heck, sometimes I do not even understand myself! I am open to second chances and try to refrain from judging. I persist, swallow the bitter pill, and push forward. The worst case is where I feel the pain again, but like any physical pain, I know I will heal and recover. Instead of teetering in the pain of rejection, consider giving the person on the other end the benefit of the doubt. Remember that most times, the rejection is not about you but rather about the situation.
- **Get up and get going again:** If I burn my finger and apply cream to help it heal, what do I do next? I don't just sit around and never cook again. I get up and continue because I need to eat. If you suffer rejection, you cannot escape the burn and pain. Follow the steps above, and then get up and

get energized to do more. Focus on your goals, and do not let this set you back, or worse still, derail you and your efforts.

> *"Be fearless. Have the courage to take risks. Go where there are no guarantees. Get out of your comfort zone, even if it means being uncomfortable. The road less traveled is sometimes fraught with barricades, bumps, and uncharted terrain. But it is on that road where your character is truly tested; have the courage to accept that you're not perfect, nothing is, and no one is—and that's OK." —Katie Couric*

Action:

Try something different to improve your communication skills. For instance, are you struggling with delivering a crucial message? Grab a piece of paper and pen and write the main message you want to pass on. What's in it for them, and how can you help? Next, practice how best to present your message: by speaking, writing, using images, or orally.

Set a goal to connect with one new person a week. Start a casual conversation on a bus ride, at church, or in the grocery store. Use these opportunities as your networking practice sessions and be genuinely interested in the person you are chatting with. It's okay if some of the connections don't go as you would like. Keep practicing and be aware that when networking formally, not every connection works out well.

When next you experience rejection, take out your journal and write down your experience, noting how you felt. Explore why you feel that way. Pour it all onto your pages. Writing has healing power, and you might discover some nuggets of wisdom from this experience.

Recap

Language barriers, employment woes, and rejection are some of the biggest hurdles an immigrant woman faces on her journey. You will experience these challenges; however, there are many things you can do to soften them, smooth your path, and flip your experiences to your advantage.

Communication is how we understand one another and are understood in turn. With a language barrier, you become limited in what you can do and achieve. You may become quiet, and your mental and emotional health may be negatively impacted.

Negotiate and navigate communication challenges through peer circles and code-switching. Embrace discomfort, reframe your experience, and magnify your interpersonal skills.

Engaging in meaningful work is desirable and worthwhile. Not having meaningful work has far-reaching negative impacts on individuals and society. You may find that your foreign credentials are not accepted, and you may have to re-skill or pivot your career direction. Although you can't control that, focus on what you can control.

Improving your job searching skills, your soft skills, and your education levels, growing your network, and establishing your career goals will improve your employability and help you navigate the challenge of getting meaningful work. Also, consider the viability of starting your own business.

You will experience rejection at least once as you scale through these hurdles. Rejection stings. Research shows that the pain of rejection is similar to the physical pain of a bad fall or a burn from the stove. However, rejection can teach you about yourself and can help you improve in many areas of your life. The key is not to take it personally. Surround yourself with love and a good social support network as you navigate these challenges, but don't deny the pain you feel and do focus on what improvements you need to make.

In the next section, we will explore how education helps immigrant women in their success journey.

Fun fact: In my handbag, I always carry my favorite photos of my family. When I encounter rejection, I pull out these photos and remind myself of those I love and who love me unconditionally. What do you have in your handbag that could help you strengthen your communication or relationships, especially when you feel challenged?

PART 3

Aligned for Success

When I joined Toastmasters International a few years ago, the first speech I was tasked with was simply talking about myself. This should be easy because we like to talk about ourselves, right? Well, it turned out not to be as easy as I imagined. What about me should I talk about? I finally settled on the question: Who am I? What would your answer be to that? Some may choose to talk about what they do and how others see them from the outside. In this book so far, I have taken you on a journey to think more deeply about your immigrant life and hopefully made you recognize that this rich path you are on has provided you with numerous opportunities to be a success in many ways. To tie all of this up and secure the foundation and frames of success you have learned so far, we will look at two overarching strategies to solidify and stabilize your journey.

Success is sequential

"Growth is never by mere chance; it is the result of forces working together." —James Cash Penney

As you go through the chapters of this book, reigniting your dream and creating transformational experiences from your challenges, it is imperative to be a lifelong learner and have financial stability. These two strongholds will position you for sustainable success in whatever you do and wherever your life journey takes you. You will get results through action. Being aware of the strategies in this book is a great first step, but if you want to see results, you need to act. By doing so, you transform yourself and your journey.

I have a question for you. Which camp do you belong to? Is it A or B?

A. You must work hard to prosper.

B. Success does not require struggling and suffering.

I don't know about you, but I really like option B. However, until recently, I subscribed to option A. How did I change this mentality? Though I cannot point to one big moment of epiphany, I can say I finally came to this realization after multiple reflections and observations and much research.

And just so you know, there's nothing terribly wrong with working hard. The problem is that some people equate "working hard" with struggle and suffering, but they are not the same.

Success can be effortless! Aligning your desires and goals with your purpose is the key to having fun while working incredibly hard to achieve success. Tell yourself this: Success can be effortless! Success is sequential!

Effortless success

I recently ran my first five-kilometer race! I ran for a cause that I am passionate about—suicide prevention. Before then, running wasn't something I aspired to. I'd rather walk. To participate in the run, I trained under different weather conditions for several months. One day stood out clearly in my mind. It was a crazy windy day. As I ran, it felt like I was pulling a truck filled with rocks. There were other periods when it felt as if I was attached to a flying kite that was gliding me along as I ran. During those times when I was pushing the truck, running against the direction of the wind, and moving with a lot of pain, I was much slower, heavier, and ran with clenched teeth. Thankfully, no one ever took any photos of me because I look much better even when I'm crying!

When I was running in the direction of the wind, my feet felt as if they were off the ground and I was floating. I didn't feel like I was exerting energy, but rather as though I was pulled by a kite. This is called going with the flow as opposed to going against the flow. This is what I also visualize as effortless success! Because though I was still running, it didn't feel like it; rather, it felt like I was moving without any effort from my end.

As an immigrant woman, your journey to effortless success involves:

    1. Recognizing your purpose: In part 1 of this book, you identified your dream, acknowledged your identity, and mapped out your path. In part 2, you explored what you have within you to help navigate the major challenges you face as an immigrant. With these strategies, you are on the path to success. However, you need a few more items in your handbag to effortlessly achieve success at all times.

2. Aligning your gifts, talents, strengths, and opportunities with your purpose: You have inherent strengths and talents that the creator bestowed on you. In addition, you have picked up a lot of valuable skills on your life journey, right from childhood. You also came into the world needing to work with others in some areas. And on top of all this, life presents you with many opportunities. You have to be open to these as well as recognizing when they are present. When you align all these—your talents, skills, opportunities, and ability to recognize what you don't have the skills for—with your purpose and goals, you get effortless success.

Effortless success is not a destination but a journey. So be aware that it's not a thing you do once and need never do again. Rather, it is something you will have to apply over and over again in many different situations.

Your definition of success is your definition alone and not someone else's. This is why you need to make sure you have aligned your goals to your purpose, so you will know when you are successful. Simply examine yourself when you are on your journey and ask the question: Does this achievement fulfill my purpose? Another way to put it would be: Is what I am working on in alignment with what I want?

Everyone wants financial stability and success. For most immigrants, this is their biggest dream. With the challenges of immigration, this dream can become a struggle, and achieving success will seem like a lot of grinding and pain.

In the next two chapters, we will talk about:

- The power of education in your walk to effortless success, and
- The path to financial stability, specifically, key areas you must not overlook.

In the last part of this book, you will put together everything you've learned in a way that will enable you to carry these tools in your handbag. My Action Plan to (effortless) Success (MAPS) will help you create your personalized roadmap to everyday success and empowerment.

CHAPTER 7

Opening Doors

"Education is the most powerful weapon, which you can use to change the world." —Nelson Mandela

When my son was a bit older and playing competitive basketball in elementary school, he was not happy about being benched frequently. He felt the coach was biased against him. Like every child, he felt he knew it all and couldn't understand how his coach was not seeing his awesomeness.

What we observed was that he would show off to his friends who came to watch the games. We realized that the reason for his anger was that when he was benched, his friends couldn't see him play. This anger began to spill into his attitude, and he was ready to quit. My husband and I sat him down and explained that to be successful, he needed to be humble and learn.

I was impressed by his enthusiasm after this chat. He watched many basketball games, learning from great players, and listened more to his coach. He also practiced in his spare time, and in a few weeks, was one of the team's star players. Children are quick to understand that to be successful, they need to learn and grow.

When I ask a group of immigrant women from around the world to name one factor that is key to their success, their top response is always education. One of the single moms I interviewed recounted how she felt imprisoned till she visited the public library and subsequently enrolled in college. In her words: "This opportunity to be in school has changed my life and my children's lives forever. I am dreaming again, and the possibilities are endless."

When she arrived in Canada, she did not speak English and was pregnant with her first child. Her family was living in a basement. Being new and with no social support system, a language challenge, and experiencing many of the issues we discussed in part two, she became "small and voiceless".

Though she had many questions to ask the gynecologist during her prenatal visits, she battled to express herself. And living in the basement without much sunlight worsened an already bad situation. Her mental health was deteriorating rapidly. Her husband, who was the only person she knew, was working two transitional low-paying jobs to make ends meet. He was hardly home. For five years, as her family grew, she remained in this situation. Then one day, she learned of the public library close by and paid a visit with her little children.

That was the beginning of her transformation. Her eyes were opened, and she was enlightened about all she could do. She slowly came out of her shell, was no longer intimidated by all her challenges, enrolled in a college to obtain language training, gained confidence, and now has a goal to have a profession in community and social services. Unfortunately, once she knew better and started pursuing her education, this caused a rift in her marriage as her partner felt threatened. They subsequently parted ways.

For some immigrant women, this example illustrates where certain cultural norms and other immigration challenges cause families to break apart during their transformational journey. This is sad and adds to the problems that many already face. However, this should not stop any woman from pursuing her education because education is your door to opportunities and a better life.

In Mandela's biography, *Long Road to Freedom* (pg. 155), he says this: "Education is the great engine of personal development. It is through education that the daughter of a peasant can become a doctor, that the son of a mineworker can become the head of the mine, that a child of a farmworker can become the president of a great nation. It is what we make out of what we have, not what we are given that separates one person from another."

Having some level of education boosts your confidence and provides a platform for you to find and use your voice, especially in important matters that impact your life. If education is, therefore, the key to success, what's your definition of education?

Being educated

What does education mean to you? There are a few definitions. Lexico defines it as "an instructive or enlightening experience."[26] Other definitions refer to education as knowledge or scholarship. It is also defined as the process of receiving or giving systematic instruction, especially at a school or a

26 https://www.lexico.com/en/definition/education

university. These definitions capture components of education, yet it is so much more. Life is a big school, and the world is the biggest playground in the school of life. I like to define education as a process, a journey that often crosses many stations including predefined destinations. It is a process where I gain academic knowledge, morals, judgment, values, wisdom, and maturity. As a life-long learner, everything, every opportunity, and every interaction is a learning experience.

Every great woman and man that ever lived never stopped learning. Their learning was not confined to the four walls of a school. They learned from others, books, and their own reflections. You cannot achieve greatness in your journey without being a student of life. For example, so far in this book, you have been learning from your own experiences as you read through the chapters and complete the relevant exercises and assessments. Therefore, it may be clear to you now that to be successful, you must have both formal and informal education.

Your education and experiences cannot be taken away from you. They're gifts that are within you, and you choose how and when you share them with the world.

Here are some of the direct benefits for immigrant women who pursue education, both formal and informal:

- **Economic power and future:** There's a strong correlation between education and higher income. Without education and good earnings, you disenfranchise yourself from power in society. Remember that education can also be informal, particularly as many successful people who have created products and movements that changed the world did not complete a university education. This does not mean they stopped learning. Rather, they learned from books, mentors, the content available on the web, and their personal experiences and mistakes. The bottom line is that you cannot make a change without knowledge. And knowledge comes from learning.

If you don't have a university education, don't be discouraged. You still have a lot to offer the world and yourself, and you can learn from books, workshops, podcasts, free courses, mentors, coaches, and simple life experiences, to name a few. By applying your learning in practical ways, you will get results. They may be small at first, but they will compound. And if it is your desire to still go to university, then go for it. If there are current barriers that are holding you back, remember you have a lot of items you can pull out of your handbag to navigate them. Begin with the dream, do some research, explore options, and start small. And if you have a university degree, remember you can stretch it to make an impact, no matter how small.

- **Personal and community impact:** The child of an educated woman gets a head start in life, which subsequently has ripple effects in the family and community. Learning opens your imagination and exposes you to different and exciting thoughts and opportunities. One big eye-opener I experienced during my research for this book was about the privilege an education affords a woman.

I was humbled to speak with many intelligent women who were denied the opportunity to share their tremendous gift with the world because of a lack of education. Their level of literacy impeded access to very key information to which, though seemingly insignificant, had they had access, could have flipped their lives around in a powerful way. Their innovative and creative solutions remain ordinary and unknown because these women remain "unseen" and do not have the right platform to be elevated. Just like the example of the friend at the beginning of this chapter, I have discovered that giving some women a little push and providing them with exposure to more knowledge makes a big difference in the outlook of their lives.

- **Better health:** Most of the benefits of having an education are interwoven. Imagine what happens when you do not know the resources available to you, or the simple preventative actions you can take for healthy living, or information about where to go for help? Sometimes this image may leave some of us thinking of only the poorest of the poor. The truth is that this lack of knowledge happens at all levels of life, both social and educational.

When I started having children, I barely took care of myself. This included periods of little personal growth. And if I read anything, it was about children. It was, therefore, no surprise that I started gaining weight, especially around my belly. For many years, I was not too bothered by this because I repeated to myself some myth about it being okay since I'd had four babies (even though I looked pregnant all the time when I wasn't). Strangely, despite how ridiculous this may sound, my belief was backed by what I had heard from some other women who said it was normal after many pregnancies.

So, I accepted my fate and didn't do more to educate myself. Many years later, after I'd busted the myth (because there were lots of women who had many babies and did not look forever pregnant), I discovered there was an actual thing called Diastasis Recti[27], and I have since started working on fixing this. Thankfully, our bodies are so great that some things correct naturally with a little help. Therefore, the point is: Don't leave your health to random myths and sources of information. Get educated!

- **Fosters stability:** With education, you learn how to take care of yourself. When you were a child, someone had to make decisions for you, but as an adult, your decisions are impacted by your levels of wisdom, knowledge, and experience. Thus, not leveraging the "school of life" and a formal education creates a disadvantage.

As girls, we may have been protected and taken care of like little princesses, and some adult women still operate like they should be taken care of by someone else. But as an immigrant woman, you must educate yourself about your finances, health, environment, etc. All of these are personal and should not be left solely in the care of someone else. In one of the interviews I conducted, one woman recounted how she'd never had to think about anything because her husband took care of her and the finances and all the other household responsibilities. Unfortunately, when their relationship broke down and they separated, she learned she had nothing to her name except debt. Her once stable life turned into a long, scary path and took a turn for the better only when she ended up in the hospital in very bad shape. She is

27 https://www.parents.com/pregnancy/my-body/postpartum/diastasis-recti-the-postpartum-body-problem-no-one-talks-about/

now an education ambassador encouraging women to get educated.

- **Bridges the inequality gap, gender violence, and child marriage:** This could simply be referred to as empowerment! In many national histories, transformation happened whenever women got involved as a massive force in any political or social justice struggle. With an education, an immigrant woman has an amplified voice. She advocates for freedom of speech and expression.

Old customs such as child marriage, not letting women vote or drive cars or go to school, along with many other injustices, are fought and abolished when women collectively raise their voices. In Mandela's *Long Walk to Freedom*, he quoted Chief Albert Luthuli: *"When women begin to take an active part in the struggle, no power on earth can stop us from achieving freedom in our lifetime."* We saw this in the Aba Riot in Eastern Nigeria (which I mentioned in the life map section in chapter 4).

These kinds of societal transformations reflect empowerment in every woman's life, and it is through education that an immigrant woman can access this power and make a positive impact on her personal life and in the community.

The lifelong learner

"Always walk through life as if you have something new to learn and you will." —Vernon Howard

You may be saying to yourself now, "Well, I don't have the time or the money to get into school." I hear you, and I know that feeling well. You may be thinking of how much work it is to find the money you need and to study for some form of education in addition to all the other sacrifices you will have to make. There's also the potential of failure. This is the reality of life; unless you make something a priority, there will always be a reason why it did not happen.

I challenge you to think differently about education. Remember that it is not restricted to academics and formal education. We are already in the big school of life. However, without focus and intentionality, this wonderful gift is wasted. You can glean a lot from life lessons and many other opportunities available to you by focusing on your personal growth and development. The journey you are on as an immigrant woman is rich soil. Educating yourself will enable that soil to expand and explode with self-confidence as you become empowered by learning.

Education is a tool that provides knowledge, skill, technique, and information. It expands your vision and outlook while enabling you to know your rights and duties in your family and the community. An educated woman is a gift to the world because, without education, she will not explore new ideas and development.

If you are skeptical about how to get an education because of time, finances, and other constraints, then let's reframe this opportunity. Explore instead the idea of being a life-long learner.

"The whole purpose of education is to turn mirrors into windows." —Sydney J. Harris

What is lifelong learning?

Lifelong learners describe themselves in many different ways. As a lifelong learner, I am always seeking and learning new things, making self-improvements, and trying out things I've never done before. As I see life through a holistic lens, I do not separate my learning journey into career and personal development. Rather, I am happy to use whatever knowledge I gain and will apply it wherever it fits.

For instance, my children have taught me patience, creativity, and the act of being curious. These are skills I had in varying degrees and used to apply in specific ways. Now, with my expanded knowledge and the wisdom I have gained through parenting, I apply these skills differently. Being an immigrant has also taught me, and continues to teach me, many new skills. Dictionary.com describes lifelong learning as "the provision or use of both **formal and informal learning opportunities** throughout people's lives to foster the **continuous development and improvement of the knowledge and skills** needed for employment and personal fulfillment."[28]

It goes on to say: "Lifelong learning is the **intentional, ongoing pursuit of knowledge** for personal or career-related reasons. **It can be formal (learning in a classroom setting) or informal (learning something from a friend, through reading, or from simple trial and error).** The concept of lifelong learning is based on the idea that classroom education is not the only form of learning. When there is no classroom (or teachers, assignments, or tests), learning must be pursued through **self-motivation.** That means having the will to learn on one's own, without

---

28 https://www.dictionary.com/browse/lifelong-learning

the supervision or demand of a teacher or other instructor." Lifelong learning is not about grades or tests. Most people want to keep learning to acquire new skills or for the simple enjoyment of learning new things.

Abraham Lincoln is a great example of a lifelong learner. He had very little formal education (about eighteen months of schooling), but he was an avid reader. He even taught himself law by reading books! Additionally, many of the world's greatest men and women never stopped learning.

The ways we learn include:

- By taking formal courses through schools.
- From experiences—ours and those of others (i.e., family, friends, mentors, coaches, and coworkers). Remember that good and bad experiences are all teaching moments in our lives.
- Going through life, we learn to adapt to new situations.
- Reading books, watching movies, and listening to podcasts/the radio.
- Deep reflection and analysis.

What does it entail to be a lifelong learner?

As we discussed earlier in this chapter, for an immigrant woman, education is necessary for success. Pursuing formal and informal education as well as being a lifelong learner will sustain effortless success in your life journey. Education is personal, and it has to be practical for it to serve you. Self-motivation is a key requirement for any kind of learning, and specifically for lifelong learning.

When you get into the habit of continuous learning, your success can start to spiral upward. You will begin to achieve extraordinary and consistent results in all aspects of your life.

You may wonder: How much work will this take? While we learn informally from our experiences, this can often be random. To make lifelong learning work for your success, you'll need focus and intention. Learning must be intentional because there is limited time and money to pursue every opportunity that presents itself. Therefore, to simplify your success journey, you need a learning plan.

The learning plan exercise

A learning plan is a tool that helps you to clearly identify your learning goals and how you will accomplish them. With a learning plan, you will see and track your progress. Below are some prompts to guide you through crafting one.

1. This is similar to the exercise in chapter one, where you will need clarity from the following questions:

◊ Where do you want to be in your career and personal life?

◊ What skills do you need in your dream life or career?

◊ Where are you at in this moment?

◊ What are you good at now?

◊ What do you need (skills or otherwise) to bridge the gap?

2. Once you figure out the skills you will need to achieve your dream, write them down in a list, **which we'll call a "skills gap list"**. (Please note that these skills can be introductory, as, depending

on your dream, you may need to start small and build upon them.)

3. Prioritize your list to identify your immediate needs and pick the one thing that will most quickly give effect to your dream.

4. Allocate timeframes for the items on your list. Learning is flexible; however, by giving your goal a set amount of time, you are more likely to accomplish it.

5. Look for and engage in only the opportunities that will help you develop those skills. You can note down other opportunities in a journal to explore later. The bottom line is that you must avoid distractions while enjoying the learning process.

6. Track your progress. This will help you to remain focused as well as pinpoint the time that you should celebrate milestones. You can use a reflective practice that I call "VNR" (Valuable, New, and Review) to check your progress in both formal and informal learning. This could take as little as five or ten minutes a week. You will need a notebook or journal to write in because, as always, writing not only provides you with records you can go back to but also helps in the reflective process.

◇ Write down one **valuable** thing you learned during the week, e.g., I learned that my sleep quality did not directly correlate with the number of hours I slept.

◇ Write down one **new** way you will use this valuable learning the following week, e.g., To improve the quality of my sleep, I will stop looking at screens one hour before bedtime.

This removes the stress of trying to increase the number of hours I sleep while improving its quality.

◇ **Review** if the planned action worked in the following week. If it did not work, ask yourself why not? As I mentioned earlier in the chapter, learning without practical application makes nonsense of the learning process.

7. Enlist accountability. Sometimes you may have good intentions, but when life happens (such as studying long hours into the night and waking up late the next day), you may get derailed, and an accountability partner is useful to get you back on track. An accountability partner is a trusted person or system that reminds you of the goal or habit you are building. Proverbs 27:17 lays it out well: "As iron sharpens iron, so one person sharpens another."

By applying this plan and following these steps, you are on your way to becoming an accomplished and successful lifelong learner!

Action:

- Draft your Learning Plan.

Recap

"A formal education will make you a living; self-education will make you a fortune." —Jim Rohn

Education, formal and informal, is an asset that cannot be taken away from you. It is your gateway to success and prosperity. By getting educated, you improve your overall well-being beyond measure.

Becoming a lifelong learner opens a flow of growth and opportunity for every woman.

"Wisdom strengthens the wise more than ten rulers of the city." —Ecclesiastes 7:19

Fun fact: My library card, which sits in the cardholder in my handbag, is my gateway to a world of discovery and learning. Check out the local library in your area; they may offer free membership or charge low membership fees.

CHAPTER 8

Money Map

"Money is only a tool. It will take you wherever you wish, but it will not replace you as the driver." —Ayn Rand

A money map is a road map or GPS that helps you identify your financial starting point and the route you need to travel to get where you want to be financially.

In the previous chapter, we established that your level of success is aided by whatever knowledge, wisdom, and actions you take. An investment in yourself through formal and informal education yields exceptional returns. As an immigrant woman, I know that money is on your mind. You may be wondering how we can talk about success without mentioning it. Most immigrants have the sole purpose of "making it" when they leave their home country for a new one. And for some, "making it" means achieving financial success.

Financial success is subjective and personal. For some people, it means being rich. And being rich may mean having a lot of money. This leads me to wonder what it means when someone says they want to have a lot of money. For the longest time, I imagined that "lots of money" was a specific number within a specified range. How about you? What is your definition of financial success? Does it translate to lots of money? And do you know what that means to you?

While I think that having money to meet one's needs and desires is part of financial success, it is much more than that. You may have heard those stories about people who come into a lot of wealth suddenly (say they win a lottery). Then, in a very short while, they are back to their starting point or even worse off. Why do you think this happens? Winning millions of dollars should make them successful, yet they blow it!

My definition of financial success includes knowing about money, having money, and doing the right things for yourself with money. Educating yourself is a must because getting a well-rounded education on money involves:

- Understanding your mindset about money,
- Understanding the workings and flow of money,
- Money management,
- How to multiply money, and
- The proper use of money as a tool for your success and the success of the community.

I love talking about money, but while I have a lot to say about it, I cannot say everything in one chapter of a book. Therefore, in this chapter, my focus will be on making a plan to attain financial stability. Financial stability is more encompassing than simply focusing on financial success because a financially stable person *is* successful. Their drive for stability is not dependent on a specific number. Rather, they work on creating a strong foundation that is sustainable for them and their family.

Living a financially stable life means you neither lack nor do you worry about meeting your needs, regardless of the economic conditions of the environment. You can make financial decisions with confidence. **Financial stability leads to financial confidence**. Who does not want that?

To have financial stability, you must build a financial system that functions during the good times and the bad. In fact, financial stability is a term used commonly by world economies and businesses. Countries and companies function through thoughtfully and well-designed systems, and so can you!

The foundational principles of financial stability

One of the antonyms of foundation is fear.[29] What comes to mind when you hear the word foundation? That's right. The foundation of a house is what typically comes to mind. Let's think of the foundational principles in terms of the foundation of a house. A house is only as stable as its foundation. If you have a shaky foundation, no matter how fancy your house is, when the elements arrive in full force it will topple and fall.

*"Therefore, everyone who hears these words of mine and puts them into practice is like **a wise man who built his house on the rock**. The rain came down, the streams rose, and the winds blew and beat against that house, **yet it did not fall because it had its foundation on the rock**. But everyone who hears these words of mine and does not put them into practice is like **a foolish man who built his house on sand**. The rain came down, the streams*

---

29 https://thesaurus.plus/related/foundation/fear

rose, and the winds blew and beat against that house, and **it fell with a great crash**." —Matthew 7:24-27 (New International Version)

The principles of financial stability never change. They are like the law of gravity. These principles apply to everyone alike regardless of age, economic class, gender, nationality, and any other differences. Though these principles can be applied in different ways to get different results, the principles themselves never change. My hope for you as you read this chapter is that (1) you know these principles of financial stability and how you may or may not have been applying them, and (2) you learn the strategies to help you establish solid financial systems that will ensure your success and financial stability. We will explore things you hear all the time. You will be challenged to think about these principles differently, and subsequently, you'll do things differently to get different results.

Money mindset

Have you ever wondered why some people come into good fortune like an inheritance, or become well-paid athletes, or win the lottery, but a few years after that, their whole fortune is gone?

The answer is simple. If someone does not have the right foundations for wealth, when they come into it, they are destined to lose it all. Why? Because they have not built the right skills, and they do not have the capacity to manage such wealth.

I had a revealing conversation with an acquaintance who had applied for and was given a new role. He was very excited to start this job because it had a lot of potential for him and the company. It was a new position in the organization, and there were lots of unknowns. It also involved overseeing a high-stakes project. Unfortunately, he recounted, he had struggled to find his footing. Though he appeared to be a good fit and had sold himself well at the interview, he discovered the skills he used to shine in his other jobs were inadequate for what was required from this new one.

He was not dishonest during the interview or in his interest in doing a good job. He just wasn't successful because he lacked the foundational skills needed to map out this brand-new role. The company also played a part by not setting him up for success as they were unclear about what they wanted from the position. In the end, this successful fellow decided to leave his job because he knew he needed different skill sets for what was required, and the deadlines for the project did not allow him enough time to develop those skills enough to deliver successfully.

This is similar to what happens with people and money. Do you live paycheck to paycheck, wondering why your best efforts do not bring you closer to financial stability? It is time to consider your mindset, specifically your money mindset.

How often do you attribute the results you get in life to your mindset? It's easier to point a finger at someplace or someone else—anywhere but ourselves. Yet, many of the results we get in life start from our mindset, including money.

What is mindset?

I'd like to focus on this definition from the Merriam-Webster dictionary, which defines it as "a **mental** inclination, tendency, or habit."[30] I have emphasized mental because most of our mindset is mental; we don't think about it, and it's not visible

30 "Mindset," Merriam-Webster (Merriam-Webster), accessed March 5, 2021, https://www.merriam-webster.com/dictionary/mindset.

to us. We just see the results in our actions, and often, we do not attribute these results to that mindset.

This leads us to money mindset.

Let's start with a quick exercise:
- Think about how you feel about money,
- Think about the phrases, words, or sentences you hear or say about money, and
- Think about the last three items you bought recently.

What feelings did these thoughts about money arouse for you? Did any negative feelings come up, or was it all positive or a mix of both?

When people have negative feelings about money, they think it's caused by a lot of things, including not having enough. But let's step back and look at these thoughts and feelings from another angle. The cognitive triangle[31] demonstrates how our thoughts influence our feelings, which, in turn, result in the actions we take. In other words, **what we think affects how we feel and act.** Let's dive deeper into this.

Your money mindset is the beliefs and attitudes you hold about your finances, and they influence all your financial decisions. Your mindset has a huge impact on the financial choices you make every day. This is why your money mindset is very important; changing it will lead to positive changes in your finances. For example, a positive mindset leads to making goals a priority and directly impacts your ability to achieve those goals.

Your mindset is mostly subconscious and has been built over time. Did your parent(s) struggle with money or spend

31 https://www.psychologytools.com/self-help/what-is-cbt/

too much of it? Were there fights in the home that were influenced by money? Did you hear things like "money does not grow on trees", "money is the root of all evil", "rich people are bad people", etc.? A lot of negative talk about money seems to float around. It is as if we neglect to be thankful for everything we are able to accomplish. **But what if you changed all these negative narratives and embraced money with a positive mindset?**

Let's walk you through what this may look like in your journey toward stability and financial success.

Relationship with money and the money mindset: If you found $10, what would you do with it? Spend it on the first thing that comes to mind, such as coffee or chocolates or random stuff? Or would you put it away? Most of us don't have a plan. We think it's free money, and subsequently, the money goes just as soon as it comes. On the other hand, if you have a budget and work with a plan, you will know where your money has gone most of the time, whether it's "free" money or not. Here's where you need to flip your thinking. **Free money could be what you save from a sale or discounted item or when you get credits to apply to expenses, etc**. Imagine what you could do with all this "free" money you don't account for. For instance, if you take all your savings from discounts and put them into your emergency fund or use them to pay off your debt, that would be intentional and a shift in your mindset.

Again, you may be wondering why your relationship with money and your money mindset matter in your financial journey. Let's look at another scenario. What are your thoughts and feelings when you hear the words "money" and "budgeting"? You should examine these feelings and thoughts that come up and really question how they impact you. For instance, if you say to yourself that you don't earn enough to save money, chances are you will never start on that journey. On the other hand, if you say to yourself that investing sounds complicated, but you will give it a try and invest twenty-five dollars a month into a mutual fund, you are more likely to start this practice.

Exploring your money mindset and your relationship with money helps you to question your actions and can lead to positive changes and habits. The power of habit compounds over time, and this goes for both good and bad habits. For example, not knowing where your money goes every month is a habit you have unconsciously formed, and you know it is a habit because it is not easy to break. To replace it, you must address the foundational mindset you have around budgeting and planning.

Steps to achieving a positive money mindset

"It is our choices that show what we truly are, far more than our abilities." —*J. K. Rowling*

Is it then possible to change these subconscious mindsets and unhealthy relationships with money? If you would like to replace a negative money mindset with a positive one, then, to tap into the full benefits of abundance, you'll need to work on your foundations. This work, though internal, will begin to transform you in many other aspects of your life. You will begin to live with purpose in accordance with your values and have consistently great success.

*"Do not be conformed to this world, but **be transformed by the renewal of your mind**, that by testing you may discern what is the will of God, what is good and acceptable and perfect."*
—*Romans 12:2 (English Standard Version)*

Awareness: Like any change and transformational work that we embark on, the first step is to know thyself. You cannot work on change if you do not first recognize that change is needed. Take some time and reflect by firstly bringing to consciousness the beliefs you currently hold. Then, question those beliefs and replace them with life-giving ones. For example:

1. Bringing your beliefs to consciousness:
Recall the statements around money that you heard while growing up, i.e., money does not grow on trees. What were your feelings about money during such discussions? Based on what you heard growing up and/or the way you feel about money generally, do you see any patterns that may be impacting your financial choices? For example, I first learned about money in a bible scripture, which taught me that "money is the root of all evil". This made me see money as a bad thing. With this ingrown and misplaced idea, I unconsciously rejected many opportunities that could have led to possessing more wealth.

My thoughts were also feeding strongly into the feelings I had around money, which in turn led me to make unconscious choices that worked against me, yet seemed to validate the fact that money was a lot of trouble. It was a wild circle, and though I worked hard, my subconscious was rejecting some legitimate ideas that would not only help me avoid financial stress but also allow me to help others. But because of my choices, I was limited and would only complain more about my money woes and how life was unfair. You see the cycle?

2. Challenge these beliefs: This can also be referred to as self-talk. Whenever I become aware that I have some strong belief about anything, or I become restless or worried, I use the TRUE framework that I introduced in the chapter on mental wellness above to challenge that belief, i.e., is it True, Right, Undeniable, and Excellent. With this blueprint, check the validity of your thoughts and discard those that don't serve you.

What beliefs do you have about money? Have you told yourself you cannot save, invest, or earn so much? How do you know that to be true? Is that really undeniably right or praiseworthy? Try saving a little amount for a week and prove those thoughts wrong.

3. Replace these thoughts with affirmations: There's a lot of power in affirmations and the words we speak. There's also no power in using positive affirmations if you subconsciously reject them on the inside. That is mental torture. We'll discuss practical ways to use affirmations to replace negative thoughts you may have held on to for years.

Now that you have brought those thoughts that may have been driving your financial choices to the forefront and also confronted them with the TRUE framework, you can use affirmations to make sure those thoughts don't rear their heads up ever again. For instance, instead of simply saying

"I am rich" or "I have zero debt" or similar, you could start with recognizing that the journey to your desired place is not perfect. As we talked about in chapter seven, you can rephrase your affirmations to flow more like this: **"Every moment, I'm making an effort to be more conscious about how I spend my money."**

This statement recognizes that your work is in progress. It also acknowledges that you have a choice in creating a better financial future for yourself. Using a statement like this will have a positive impact on your money decisions, and that is so much better than saying, "I am rich."

Here's my challenge for you right now. Stop reading and say out loud the following affirmation. **"Every moment, I'm making an effort to be more conscious about how I spend my money."** Notice how you feel as opposed to when you say, "I have zero debt." Regularly repeating affirmations like this starts to imprint an image that is aligned with the affirmation, and as a result, you will find yourself making empowering choices around money. Try it!

Money habits

"Only 20% of personal financial success is head knowledge, the other 80% is behavior." —Dave Ramsey[32]

You are now conscious of some of the underlying drivers behind your relationship with money. You recognize and acknowledge that this impacts the way you feel about money and also illustrates some of the habits you have been creating in your personal finances.

32 Dave Ramsey Quotes. BrainyQuote.com, BrainyMedia Inc, 2021. https://www.brainyquote.com/quotes/dave_ramsey_520281, accessed March 4, 2021.

The next step in having a strong foundation involves creating good, solid money habits. While your mindset is the foundation, your habits are your building's framework. When you think of a house being constructed, the foundation is a critical element in the building process because it holds up the entire structure. It must be constructed correctly to prevent future problems that can affect the home's safety and efficiency.

After the foundation is poured and set, the framing of the house begins. Just as our skeleton serves as the structure for our bodies, the framework of a house is the underlying structure of the home. The framework helps you identify the doors, windows, rooms, hallways, etc. With this image in mind, let us go back to your financial stability. If your mindset is faulty, then even with the right money habits, your financial stability is compromised because you will sabotage your efforts. Likewise, having a positive money mindset and poor money habits is useless because the structure will collapse even though its foundation stands firm. This could lead to an unending cycle of raising the frame only to have the same result. For example, someone who knows the right choices to make about their finances but spends more than they earn cannot progress much.

Humans are creatures of habit, and we do a lot of things out of habit. Conversely, we also do *not* do a lot of things out of habit. Thus, inaction is also a habit because any decision or action you constantly do not take becomes a habit you practice.

Many people are afraid to look at their finances for different reasons. It could be that they don't know how to take care of their money, that they are afraid of the debt they have accumulated, or that they cannot fulfill the basic needs of their families. Since this inaction is a habit and may not be working for you, why not replace your approach with some healthier, wealthier money habits? Find these out below.

Healthy, wealthy money habits

"Poor spending habits lead to poverty"
—Mac Duke, The Strategist[33]

Such habits include:

• **Set money goals:** These could be short-term, mid-term, and long-term goals. What are the things needing money that you want to achieve at these different stages? How much income would you like to have in the short term, midterm, and long term? Write these out and include them in your financial plan.

• **Identify your values:** What are your values? Your values should be the big influencer of your spending. When people have not identified their values, their spending is often swayed by whatever someone else is buying or doing. This is often referred to as "keeping up with the Joneses".[34] This is a slippery slope for immigrants who might want to show that they are successful by adopting other people's appearance of success.

• **Take the driver's seat in your money matters:** It is called "personal finance" because it is personal. No one will take care of your money in the

---

33 "Mac Duke The Strategist Quotes," Goodreads (Goodreads), accessed March 5, 2021, https://www.goodreads.com/author/quotes/18036498.Mac_Duke_The_Strategist.
34 https://www.merriam-webster.com/dictionary/keep%20up%20with%20the%20Joneses

way that works best for you, except you. Of course, you can delegate certain aspects of your finances to trusted people, but you'll need to know what they are doing and ensure it's in alignment with where you are going.

• **Invest in you:** This includes investing time, energy, and money in your personal growth, i.e., learning new skills and being well and healthy. Learn about tax planning. Educate yourself about banking, investments, and insurance. Not only will you get better educated about your personal finances, but you will also increase your skills and earning potential.

• **Build and fund your emergency purse:** Life always happens. Having cash set aside that is easily accessible will save a lot of stress when—and not if—something unforeseen happens. The dictionary definition of an emergency is a serious, unexpected, and often dangerous situation requiring immediate action.[35] Forgetting to pay a bill or desiring to get some item on sale is not an emergency. Your computer crashing during online schooling is an emergency, however.

• **Budget, budget, budget:** Know how much you make and where your money is going. You cannot make any meaningful changes if you don't know where the leaks are or what to do to patch the leak. Creating and maintaining a budget will reveal your spending habits, saving habits, and money-making mindset. A budget is a basic and fundamental tool for successful money management. Do not be deceived

---

35 https://www.lexico.com/definition/emergency

by saying you know what you make and where it goes. Writing it out and planning the inflows and outflows is the best way to determine what is actually going on. There are no successful businesses that operate without a budget, a forecast, and financial statements. This is not any different for you as an individual either, as your budget, expense tracking, and money goals operate under the same process.

• **Monitor your systems:** Check your accounts regularly. Understand your pay stub or payslip. Understand your bills. Sometimes, mistakes happen with transactions. By checking your accounts, budget, bills, pay stubs, banks, investments, and other insurance statements regularly, you will catch any leaks that may happen, including unnecessary charges, fees, and errors.

Optimizing your money habits

The truth is that most women who are taking care of others and not earning much of a wage already do their best with managing and stretching their dollars. The idea of creating healthy, wealthy money habits is to take these skills you already have to the next level. By being strategic and intentional in these best practices, you can automate. Your mental headspace will be freed up, reducing the stress involved in thinking about how tight things are. Instead, your money will work effortlessly for you.

Embrace the following:

• Autosave monthly. Many banks have this feature with their accounts. Use it.

- Check your accounts every other day. With online banking and mobile apps, this takes only a few minutes. You can also set up reminders in your calendar for this task.
- Have a budget. Enough said already!
- Have financial goals that you are working on. This also gives you a reason to celebrate as you accomplish them.
- Pay off your credit card in full every month. I've provided more on credit cards in the section below.
- Set up all your bills to be paid automatically and align them with when you receive your paycheck.
- Invest every month. Every woman should know about investing her money. As little as twenty-five dollars a month adds up.
- Read or listen to some material on personal finance. Education is power!
- Do your estate planning. As you build wealth, do not neglect to minimize some financial risks that may occur. Estate planning includes planning for death and incapacity when you cannot speak for yourself. Buy life and disability insurance, make sure to write a will, and apply a personal directive and a power of attorney. A will stipulates your last wishes and how you would like your assets shared out when you die. In the case of incapacitation due to a mental or physical situation (i.e., if you experience a stroke), a power of attorney gives the attorney rights to make financial decisions on your behalf, while a personal directive gives the person named in the document the rights to make decisions regarding your health and other personal matters that are non-financial.

While these are uncomfortable things to discuss, they are key to your financial stability.

To create a habit, you have to practice it repeatedly until that memory muscle is trained to do the action without thinking, i.e., like brushing your teeth. It is more challenging to break an old habit, especially those not working in your favor. Here are some tips to creating healthy, wealthy habits:

1. Start small. Choose one thing that will impact many other areas, e.g., I choose to focus on my grocery spending, and I decide to use only cash to pay for them. This may lead me to meal planning and getting creative with items already in my pantry. It will lead me to stop or reduce food wastage by buying only what I need. It may also lead me to eat healthier, and before long, this will transfer to other areas of my life.

2. Create a schedule. There is no need to use someone else's schedule. Create one that works for you and that you will use because it aligns with your values and goals.

3. Be consistent. Consistency is key, and it has been proven that repeating an action for at least thirty days can lead to creating a habit. However, if you break the chain for one day, just pick up where you left off the following day.

4. Focus on small progressions. A little drop will finally make a mighty ocean. Every bit of savings will compound, and though we may not see it initially, it does build up over time, e.g., saving twenty-five dollars a month becomes $250.00 in ten months, which is $250.00 you would not have if you had never started. Thus, it's important to remain focused.

5. Build in accountability. Use a calendar or find a person or a group to help keep you accountable. You could also start a blog about your journey, post on social media about what you are doing, or just announce it to your loved ones. Your progress usually works to motivate you and your friends, and your family will help you continue that progress.

6. Finally, don't beat yourself up if you get off track. Just get up and get back on track. Anything you do at all, no matter how small, is moving you forward, not backward. If you don't pick yourself up but continue to shy away, you are not just static; you are losing whatever progress you may have made.

Above, we covered the key fundamental principles for financial stability. As some immigrant women may be new to using credit or didn't learn the facts about credit before they started using it, I will address this in more detail below.

Credit

"Just as the rich rule the poor, so the borrower is servant to the lender." —Proverbs 22:7 (New Living Translation)

Credit is debt, and minimizing debt is a rule of Bible economics.

When I was growing up in Nigeria, owning a property meant you owned it whole and entire. The cultural values were such that transactions were solely cash-based, and if anyone didn't have cash, they would borrow from people they knew. These transactions were more or less based on honor systems. They could also trade by barter, and there were a few money lenders as well. Credit was different as it was used mostly by businesses.

When I lived in Italy, I found similar values where credit was used for very big transactions like buying a home, business investments, and for items that were not "everyday". In Canada, things are very different. Credit is elevated. People get introduced to the convenience of credit, often without any education on what credit is or the best practices for using it. People are so uninformed that they become trapped and remain trapped while the lenders continue to make money off this ignorance and financial stress. Interestingly, it's not only individuals who fall into this credit trap. Organizations and even nations are so indebted that generations yet to come are already mortgaged.

It would be great to adopt some of the values on credit from those days in Nigeria and Italy, but the truth is that once in certain countries, credit is in your face, and it's best to know how to use it and what you need so that as the scripture above says, you don't find yourself a servant of the lender.

In this section, we will explore credit, including:

- What is credit
- The types of credit
- If you need credit
- How credit works
- How to manage credit well, including your options for credit and how to keep yourself informed.

What is credit?

"Every time you borrow money, you're robbing your future self." —Nathan W. Morris[36]

My definition of credit is the ability to borrow money or <u>gain access to</u> services and goods with an understanding

36 https://www.goodreads.com/quotes/639632-every-time-you-borrow-money-you-re-robbing-your-future-self

that you will pay it back in the future. Credit = Debt because you are owing something or somebody. Thus, it's important to note the key words **owe** versus **own.** This is what I find troubling in a credit-based culture. The convenience that credit provides and the ease of obtaining it leads to the false belief that people who are in serious debt own properties and goods or services while the reverse is the reality. They are owe-ers, not owners.

Creditors are **lenders** (usually via a bank or financial institution), **service providers** (phone, electricity, internet providers), and **merchants** (where you buy cars, or items online or from a store). Creditors give you credit based on their confidence level that you will pay back not only the money they gave you but also any interest or finance charges that may be applicable. If you have **good credit**, creditors will have more confidence in granting you more credit.

What is good credit?

When you think of loans from friends and family, your reputation is what determines how "creditworthy" you are. However, to obtain loans from banks and service providers, your **credit history** is what helps lenders and creditors determine your creditworthiness without bias and manipulation. Your credit history is a record of your borrowing and repaying trends, and it is summarized in files known as **credit reports**. These are compiled by independent credit bureaus like TransUnion and Equifax. Banks, credit unions, credit card issuers, and other creditors voluntarily report your borrowing and repayment information to the credit bureaus.

What is in your credit report?

Your credit report provides the following information:
- The number of credit card accounts you have, their borrowing limits, and current outstanding balances,
- The amounts of any loans you've taken out and how much of them you've paid back,
- Whether your monthly payments for your accounts were made on time, late, or missed altogether, and
- More severe financial setbacks such as mortgage foreclosures, car repossessions, and bankruptcies.

To help narrow their lending decisions, creditors often use a three-digit number known as a **credit score,** and this is their first step in deciding whether or not to issue you credit. Your credit score is recorded on your credit reports and minimizes the possibility of bias since the lenders do not personally know you.

The higher your credit scores, the more creditworthy you are. That is what good credit means. And while knowing you may not be able to escape from using credit, it's important to understand that your ability to borrow is dependent on your borrowing and repayment history, all of which gets calculated as your credit score on your credit report.

Why do I say you may not escape credit altogether? Well, while it is possible to go without credit, credit is not altogether a problem. Just like money, it is a tool. And a tool should not create more stress in your life; it should help you enjoy life. Below are some examples of credit. You will notice from the list that credit is common; however, the misuse of credit (whether due to a lack of knowledge or the trap of convenience and living above one's means) is a big problem for individuals and communities.

- Phone, internet, and utility bills: These bills are usually charged after the service has been used. The service providers supply the services with the understanding that you will pay at the end of the billing cycle. To make sure your credit remains good, you must not default on the payment of these bills. However, if you are struggling to make payments for whatever reason, it is best to connect with the service provider and work out a plan.
- Shopping bills paid with credit cards: The credit card is one of the biggest means of credit access that people have. Unlike holding credit with service providers, credit cards allow you to spend future money today, i.e., you are spending money you have not yet earned. Some credit card expenses include online shopping, shopping in the malls, buying vacation packages, and tickets to different things and places. While these expenses are not bad, especially if it is within your means, chances are, if you were to pay cash for some of these expenses, you would probably not buy them. If you are struggling with this (and it is a big struggle for most of us), there are many strategies you can use to minimize this kind of spending. You could choose to ask yourself whether you would buy the item or package if you had to pay cash. You could also go shopping with only cash in your handbag. Having an accountability partner can also help you check some of these impulses. Lastly, I recommend you do not get too many credit cards.

You do not need all of them, and if required, one or two cards will be sufficient.

• Loans: Most people are familiar with this type of credit as it's one of the oldest forms. Car loans, student loans, mortgages, and business and personal loans are good examples. When you get a loan, you end up paying back the amount borrowed in a number of installments with interest and fees applied over an agreed-upon period.

Credit or no credit

Do you need credit? It's often challenging to make a good case for debt. Some people say there's good debt and bad debt. I like simply to call it debt, as calling debt "good" may justify the need to keep oneself indebted. There are always options to get what we want. If you set a value that focuses on maintaining minimal or zero debt, it opens you up to other options on accessing what you need or want without going into debt. While this is not always easy or obvious, many people go for the fast and easy, which ultimately impacts the quality of their lives as they become bogged down by debt. Certain debt, like a mortgage that involves a huge sum of money and low interest, may be categorized as good debt by many financial gurus. However, there are a lot of options available to pay this type of debt off quickly, but without focus and intentionality, many immigrants fall into paying higher mortgages for longer.

So, going back to the question of whether one needs credit or not, it really depends. And knowing that it's almost impossible not to be bombarded with credit, it's best to be informed about what you are getting into should you choose to get some. Credit is sold and solicited on campuses to young adults who have no source of income or any education about how to use it. Credit is sold by banks and merchants who make enticing offers with increasing credit limits. It is only by understanding the psychology involved in this culture, and which remains rooted in your values (see the work you've already done on your money mindset above), that you can truly answer this question for yourself.

In summary:

1. Technically, to borrow money for any major purchase like a home, one needs to have **good credit.**

2. There are a host of others aside from lenders who may require your credit score and credit reports to do business with you. These include:

A. Landlords who check your credit when deciding whether to rent you an apartment or when determining how large the security deposit should be.

B. Insurance companies, which use your credit scores to determine your rates.

C. Utility companies that check your credit before you open an account or borrow equipment.

D. Prospective employers who may use the information found in credit reports to make a hiring decision.

Should you choose to get and use credit, here are ways you can build your credit history and maintain a high credit score. These include:

- If you are new to a country and have no credit history, get a secured credit card. With a secured credit card, you put down your own money on the card, which provides you the same services and interest charges as any other credit card. If you have a partner and you are a secondary cardholder on their account, note that this builds their credit history, not yours. A secure credit card is an option for anyone not yet working who wants to start building their credit. They can charge their cell phone bills to this card and **pay it in full monthly**.

• Pay your service provider bills with your credit card. You need discipline to use a credit card for paying bills and other expenses. The idea here is that since you will be paying these bills regularly, you may decide to set up the payments to go through your credit card. But do not stop there! You need to set up automatic transfers from your bank account to pay it off in full. This hits two targets with one arrow. The service provider reports that you pay your bills on time, and the credit card statements report that you pay off your credit on time.

• To use this system for your benefit, you must take a few crucial steps, including:

1. Negotiate your contract and get the best service for your current needs.

2. Negotiate a budget payment plan. Some service providers prorate your annual payment into twelve equal monthly payments. This helps with your budget.

3. Get the billing cycle to match when you receive any inflows (i.e., paycheck, government cheques for credits, any regular income).

4. Set up an automatic payment to service your credit card bill before the due date.

• If, for some reason, you are not able to pay any bill when due, make sure to talk with the service provider/lender to work out a plan so that your record is not negatively impacted. If you need professional assistance, undergo credit counseling.

Debt is one of the biggest things that can destabilize you financially, so make sure always to understand the terms and conditions of any contracts or loans you are going into.

Action:

- Answer the money mindset questions to determine what drives your money actions and results.
- Create one healthy, wealthy money habit. Start with weekly tracking of your expenses.

Recap

"Empty pockets never held anyone back. Only empty heads and empty hearts can do that." —Norman Vincent Peale[37]

Financial stability is the roadmap to your financial freedom and independence. Financial stability means you can cover all your bills, build wealth, and enjoy life.

The first point on your money roadmap is determining your money mindset. A positive money mindset influences your money choices.

Once you identify and build a positive money mindset, you then create healthy, wealthy money habits. These habits will ensure that you are on track to being financially stable.

37 Norman Vincent Peale Quotes. BrainyQuote.com, BrainyMedia Inc, 2021. https://www.brainyquote.com/quotes/norman_vincent_peale_106832, accessed March 4, 2021.

Get educated about credit. Being in debt increases your stress and impedes your success.

Fun fact: I keep a laminated red card beside my credit card. This little red card is titled, "Stop, look & listen." It asks these questions:

- Do I WANT or NEED this?
- Am I buying this ONLY because it's on sale?
- Would I buy this if I had to pay cash?
- Am I buying this because I'm upset?
- Would I be happy if I bought this tomorrow?
- If I charge this to my credit card, will I be able to pay it off in full by the end of the month?
- How else can I make myself feel better NOW?

CHAPTER 9

Let Your Light Shine

"Change the way you look at things and the things you look at will change." —Wayne Dyer[38]

Congratulations! You've put into your handbag all the vital items you'll need for any adventure. I hope that going through this book has provided insights and jazzed up your confidence in your life journey as an immigrant woman. You are now equipped and empowered as you experience transformations in your immigrant life.

Change is constant, and immigration provides you an excellent opportunity for transforming any change you encounter. To make sure this beautiful opportunity is not wasted, you must be intentional and learn from your unique experiences. I have provided a guiding post and many frameworks to use on your journey by turning the immigration experience into strategies for success.

38 Dyer, Dr Wayne. *Power of Intention: Change the Way You Look at Things and the Things You Look at Will Change.* Hay House UK Ltd, 2004.

These eight strategies, whether implemented individually or grouped together, will empower you to confidently negotiate challenges and achieve effortless success in your endeavors. You may regard them as your personal MAPS: My(yours really) Action Plan to (Effortless) Success, keeping them close to you in your handbag as you go on the journey of life. I have recapped them below:

1. Clarity: "Where are you going?" This is the question I asked myself fairly often as I prepared to leave my home country for the first time. The same question that was echoed by the passenger sitting next to me the night I flew out of my country. And it is the same question I often ask myself as my life takes a new turn. This question is powerful. You may be struggling to find those answers now, or you may have found them already. Regardless, you now know that the opportunity provided to you by immigration is a powerful one as it is a means by which you are transformed. The power lies in being intentional as you go through many transformations, and this question provides clarity on where and why you are going with that change. It also helps you navigate the journey with purpose and meaning, which ultimately leads to success.

2. Self-identity: As an immigrant woman, you stand tall and bold because you know your identity. You know who you are and what you are made of. All the elements of your journey from childhood to date make up your life map and the stories of the people that have gone before you. These propel you to continued success and greatness. Don't shy away from discovering who you are by NOT unwrapping that beautiful gift. Share it with the world. The seasons in your life may temporarily cause you to lose yourself, but they only help refine and shape who you already are. Finding yourself through little acts and moments will embolden you as you take the next step on your journey.

3. The driver: You blaze the trails you cross because you have a plan for the transitions that lead you to transformation. Your experiences have equipped you with excellent knowledge on how to plan transitions and map your path. Even with those moments of tough questions and choices, you are in the driver's seat because you know where you are going and what you want. As a driver, you are in charge of what roads to take, what detours to make, and the location of your final destination. Being anchored in a higher power enables you to always find your bearings no matter what is thrown at you.

4. Acculturated: There are many challenges on your journey, and you have thought of these beforehand, coming up with options of addressing these by using "what if" scenarios. This enables you to learn from others and yourself. You see opportunities and recognize when a challenge you've anticipated is facing you. You know how to mitigate or minimize them, and you empathize with others sharing similar journeys because you have transcended multi-cultural barriers.

5. Communicator: You are a champion as you navigate with pride and excellence through the barriers of language, be it spoken, written, or non-verbal. You use your position as an immigrant woman to negotiate situations as you employ your rich language skills, including signs, drawing, and vocalizing. You are a global citizen who can empathize with others because you know and understand their languages, both spoken and unspoken.

6. Healthy you: You are strong and resilient, speaking up and speaking out about mental health and wellness for yourself and others. You have items in your handbag to re-center and align yourself to success when a shift happens. You are not afraid to seek help and support when needed. Knowing that mental health is for everyone dispels any shame or stigma you feel.

7. Educated: You radiate success, pulling out the right items from your handbag at the right moments to establish yourself in the home, workplace, and community. You've got a world-class education from different parts of the world, and the unique perspectives you offer in the home, workplace, and community are precious.

8. Money magnet: You attract money because you appreciate money and use it as a tool. You have a positive money mindset that empowers you to make good money choices. You create healthy, wealthy habits that you consistently keep as you progress toward financial stability and freedom. Being well-informed about money, money management, investment, estate planning, and credit promotes your wellbeing. With the right financial tools and systems, you can leverage opportunities and have options in decision-making.

"It takes as much energy to wish as it does to plan."
—*Eleanor Roosevelt*

Immigration is a bold step. It comes with challenges, pains, joys, and successes. It is a gift that leaves you transformed. Through this book, it is my hope that you can set aside some time to reflect and learn intentionally from your story. The stories we tell ourselves, both consciously and unconsciously, are powerful. This book will be more potent and beneficial if you choose to act on any of the eight strategies we've discussed. You are after all, a courageous woman.

Living hope

"Consult not your fears but your hopes and your dreams. Think not about your frustrations but about your unful- filled potential. Concern yourself not with what you tried and failed at, but with what it is still possible for you to do." —*Pope John XXIII*

ACKNOWLEDGMENTS

I often get excited and have lots of ideas. Writing a book is not possible with just having an idea. There are many people who helped me all the way and I'd like to acknowledge them.

First, I am thankful to God Almighty without whom all of this will not be.

I am indebted to my loving husband, Ugo for his incredible support and love. You are a big part of why we have a finished book. You listened patiently with the many ideas I always came up with, asking me those critical questions to help me figure out which direction to take. You are very supportive of my huge time and financial commitments to learning and writing. You cooked meals for the household for many months unending, constantly checking in on my progress especially those times I was ready to quit. You are my biggest fan, telling all your friends about your "author" wife and pre-selling copies, reading my first draft and reminding me not to take on too much while making sure I had little to worry about. Even while dealing with the loss of your loving mom (RIP) along with many other struggles, you remained very selfless in your love and support. I love you! Thank you!

Hugs and kisses to my children, Aggie, Cristie, Cate & Emmanuel who inspire and teach me daily through your interesting and rich outlook of life. You are a fun bunch. You are all turning out alright – thank God! Love you lots.

Mom & dad, the biggest encouragers ever – you always shower me with your blessings, I appreciate and love you immensely.

My sisters, Chi & Amaka, you are a big part of why I chose to write on this topic of successful immigrant women–your journeys as strong women and our loss of Bismarck (RIP) reminds me to look for the beauty in life. Precious!

Special thanks to my brothers, Obinna, Olisa & Vic – my brother-in-law – I always have a good laugh whenever we connect and some of them lead me to reminisce about our childhood. You guys each have a big heart!

To my nieces & nephews – Chimdi, Amanda O., Ketandu, Chiazor, Amanda N., Ahamdi, Ogemdi, Nelo, Chisom, Kene, Ethan, Luke, Chloe & Levi–If you get to read this book, you will be in awe of your dear parents.

You know those people that have a big impact in your life anytime you interact with them? What could I accomplish without you all? I am very grateful to:

Debbie who has such a giving heart always looking out for me, my family and the children – even when I forget to get them gifts when there's a celebration, Debbie, Bec and family, I'm always thinking of you. Gene – you are family and your passion in any endeavor encouraged me to go for it. Arlayna & Heather, amazing friends who always check up on me, hang out with me, ask about my progress and share resources. You are the best. Cathy, thanks for always checking in. Dave & Bruno, I can always count on you – always asking how you can help, showing me the way from your wealth of experiences and connecting me with people and resources. Ritchard, you believed in me and reminded me of my own success story and that it was worth telling so others can be encouraged. Ritchard once said to me, never sell yourself short or undervalue yourself. Pastor Olawunmi, my transformational coach who reminds me that God has given it all to me already, I only need to see it and become it. Dr. Chinwe & Kiki, my accountability partners who challenged me to START. Thanks team! Joy—you enlightened me on many aspects of mental health and wellness, reading my first draft on the mental health chapter – I appreciate you. Petrina, you encourage me, teaching me efficient and productive ways to manage my time, showing me options and resources including how to get comfortable with social media and always checking-in. Many blessings girlfriend! Yenni, you once said to me, "you are a great writer so just do it". I've done it! Joanne, you always have a listening ear, helping me think things through. We go a long way. Liza and Sean, my mentors who groomed me on my professional journey and always listen when I reach out. Thank you.

To the many women and men whom I interviewed, worked with, completed my survey and supported me in various ways—Chinenye, Unoo, Nnenna E., Eka, Nelo, Nusrat, Heejung, Kelty, Amanda, Mandi, Vicky, Hana, Marjorie, Alix, my friends at DMA Global, Esther, Tolu, Moji, Pamela, Yemisi, Elsie, Comfort, Titi, Amaka U., Shola, Mae, Ope, Joyce, Charu, Chioma N., Esther E., and so many others I am not unable to name—your insights, stories and responses were powerful reminders of the transformational journey immigrant women go through and the many shades of success and confidence

To Mrs. Mesigo – our adopted mother in Canada for your care and love.

To my entire book production team—editors, formatters, and cover design team, my coaches and self -publishing school team – Corina, Joy S., Joris, Danijela, Suzanna, the team at Cutting Edge Studios – who shared their expertise and patiently walked me through what I needed at every stage of my writing and book production process

To my sisters in the Super Abundant Women group – amazing community of God-fearing women who share their gifts selflessly and spur each other on.

To our dear friends in Italy: Mauricio, Antonella, Anna Maria, Fabiana, Maria, Giovani, Doro, Nicola, Roberto – you were a big part of our sojourn in a new land. Your patience and loving acceptance as we learned and your eagerness in sharing your homes and love was a perfect model of caring for the foreigner. Grazie mille amici noi. Tante baci!

To everyone who has prayed for me, taught me in any way and said positive things to me and about me – THANK YOU!

BIBLIOGRAPHY

"Encyclopedia of Western Colonialism since 1450. Encyclopedia.com." Encyclopedia.com. Accessed February 25, 2021. https://www.encyclopedia.com/history/encyclopedias-almanacs-transcripts-and-maps/igbo-womens-war.

"Encyclopedia of Western Colonialism since 1450. Encyclopedia.com." Encyclopedia.com. Accessed February 25, 2021. https://www.encyclopedia.com/history/encyclopedias-almanacs-transcripts-and-maps/warrant-chiefs-africa.

Adelman, Mara B. "Cross-Cultural Adjustment." International Journal of Intercultural Relations 12, no. 3 (1988): 183–204. https://doi.org/10.1016/0147-1767(88)90015-6.

Bauder, Harald. "'Brain Abuse', or the Devaluation of Immigrant Labour in Canada." Antipode 35, no. 4 (2003): 699–717. https://doi.org/10.1046/j.1467-8330.2003.00346.x.

"Bridges Transition Model." William Bridges Associates, March 12, 2020. https://wmbridges.com/about/what-is-transition/#:~:text=Transition%20starts%20with%20an%20ending,and%20what%20they%20will%20keep.

Bridges, William, Susan Bridges, and Michael Bungay Stanier. Transitions: Making Sense of Life's Changes. New York, NY: Lifelong Books, an imprint of Perseus Books, LLC, 2019.

Burrus, Daniel. The Anticipatory Organization: Turn Disruption and Change into Opportunity and Advantage. Austin, TX: Greenleaf Book Group Press, 2017.

Cassar, Joanne, and Michelle Attard Tonna. "They Forget That I'm There: Migrant Students Traversing Language Barriers at School." IAFOR Journal of Language Learning 4, no. 1 (2019). https://doi.org/10.22492/ijll.4.1.01.

"Culture Shock." Dictionary.com. Accessed March 5, 2021. https://www.dictionary.com/browse/culture-shock#:~:text-t=a%20state%20of%20bewilderment%20and,foreign%20social%20and%20cultural%20environment.

Cyrulnik, Boris. "Resilience, Mental Health, and Migrations." Mental Health, Mental Illness and Migration (2018), 1–9. https://doi.org/10.1007/978-981-10-0750-7_14-1.

Deschene, Lori. Tiny Buddha: Simple Wisdom for Life's Hard Questions. Summer Hill, N.S.W.: Rockpool Publishing, 2018.

Dubin, Alesandra. "Diastasis Recti: The Postpartum Body Problem No One Talks About." Parents (May 26, 2015). https://www.parents.com/pregnancy/my-body/postpartum/diastasis-recti-the-postpartum-body-problem-no-one-talks-about/.

Dyer, Dr Wayne. Power of Intention: Change the Way You Look at Things and the Things You Look at Will Change. Hay House UK Ltd, 2004.

"Education: Definition of Education." Oxford Dictionary on Lexico.com. Also "Meaning of Education." Lexico Dictionaries | English. Lexico Dictionaries. Both accessed February 25, 2021. https://www.lexico.com/en/definition/education.

Eker, T. Harv. Secrets of the Millionaire Mind in Turbulent Times. New York, NY: Harper Audio, 2005.

Ellison, Ralph. Invisible Man. Brantford, Ontario: W. Ross MacDonald School Resource Services Library, 2018.

"EMERGENCY: Definition of EMERGENCY." Oxford Dictionary on Lexico.com. Also "Meaning of EMERGENCY." Lexico Dictionaries | English. Lexico Dictionaries. Both accessed March 5, 2021. https://www.lexico.com/definition/emergency.

Employment and Immigration Canada. "Extracts from the Annual Report 1982-83, Employment and Immigration Canada." Refuge: Canada's Journal on Refugees (1983), 20. https://doi.org/10.25071/1920-7336.21098.

"Foundation and Fear Are Antonyms." Thesaurus.plus. Accessed February 25, 2021. https://thesaurus.plus/related/foundation/fear.

Gollwitzer, Peter M. "Weakness of the Will: Is a Quick Fix Possible?" Motivation and Emotion 38, no. 3 (June 3, 2014): 305–22. https://doi.org/10.1007/s11031-014-9416-3.

Hayward, Robert, and Paul Cutler. "What Contribution Can Ordinary People Make to National Mental Health Policies?" Community Mental Health Journal 43, no. 5 (2007): 517–26. https://doi.org/10.1007/s10597-007-9086-7.

Herrman, Helen, Shekhar Saxena, and Rob Moodie. "WHO Global Project: Promoting Mental Health: Concepts, Emerging Evidence, Practice." PsycEXTRA Dataset (2004). https://doi.org/10.1037/e538802013-009.

"If Your Only Tool Is a Hammer Then Every Problem Looks Like a Nail." Quote Investigator. Accessed January 11, 2019. https://quoteinvestigator.com/2014/05/08/hammer-nail/.

"Intersectionality." Merriam-Webster. Accessed February 25, 2021. https://www.merriam-webster.com/dictionary/intersectionality.

IWPR analysis of American Community Survey microdata (Integrated Public Use Microdata Series, Version 5.0). "Spotlight on Immigrant Women: Poverty & Opportunity Data." Women in the States (July 29, 2015). https://statusofwomendata.org/spotlight-on-immigrant-women-poverty-opportunity-data/.

"John Barrow Quotes." BrainyQuote. Xplore. Accessed February 24, 2021. https://www.brainyquote.com/quotes/john_barrow_234812.

Jones, Benjamin. "What Is Code-Switching?" Dictionary. com. Accessed January 19, 2021. https://www.dictionary. com/e/code-switching/.

Kaur, Hardeep, and Matthew Whalley. "What Is Cognitive Behavioral Therapy (CBT)?" Psychology Tools (July 5, 2020). https://www.psychologytools.com/self-help/what-is-cbt/.

"Keep Up With The Joneses." Merriam-Webster. Accessed February 25, 2021. https://www.merriam-webster.com/ dictionary/keep%20up%20with%20the%20Joneses.

Keller, Gary, and Jay Papasan. The One Thing: The Surprisingly Simple Truth behind Extraordinary Results. Austin, TX: Bard Press, 2017.

Keyes, Corey L. "Promoting and Protecting Mental Health as Flourishing: A Complementary Strategy for Improving National Mental Health." American Psychologist 62, no. 2 (2007): 95–108. https://doi.org/10.1037/0003-066x.62.2.95.

"Lifelong Learning." Dictionary.com. Accessed February 25, 2021. https://www.dictionary.com/browse/ lifelong-learning.

"Mac Duke The Strategist Quotes." Goodreads. March 5, 2021. https://www.goodreads.com/author/quotes/18036498. Mac_Duke_The_Strategist.

Mandela, Nelson. Long Walk to Freedom: the Autobiography of Nelson Mandela with Connections. Austin, TX: Holt, Rinehart and Winston, 2000.

"Mental Illness and Addiction: Facts and Statistics." CAMH. Accessed February 25, 2021. https://www.camh.ca/en/driving-change/the-crisis-is-real/mental-health-statistics.

"Mindset." Merriam-Webster. Accessed March 5, 2021. https://www.merriam-webster.com/dictionary/mindset.

Morris, Claire. "How Language Barriers Amplify Power Imbalances in Migrant Camps." We Are Restless (2020). https://wearerestless.org/2020/10/02/how-language-barriers-amplify-power-imbalances-in-migrant-camps/.

"Self-Identity: Definition of Self-Identity." Oxford Dictionary on Lexico.com. Also "Meaning of Self-Identity." Lexico Dictionaries | English. Lexico Dictionaries. Both accessed March 4, 2021. https://www.lexico.com/definition/self-identity.

"Shell Scenarios." Shell Global. Accessed February 25, 2021. https://www.shell.com/energy-and-innovation/the-energy-future/scenarios.html.

"Shock: Definition of Shock." Oxford Dictionary on Lexico.com. Also "Meaning of Shock." Lexico Dictionaries | English. Lexico Dictionaries. Both accessed March 5, 2021. https://www.lexico.com/definition/shock.

Smetanin, P, D Stiff, C Briante, C E Adair, S Ahmad, and M Khan. "Mental Health Commission of Canada Releases Guidelines for Comprehensive Mental Health Services for Older Adults in Canada." PsycEXTRA Dataset, 2011. https://doi.org/10.1037/e505332013-001.

Spitzer, Denise L. "4. Policy (In)Action: Policy-Making, Health, and Migrant Women." Racialized Migrant Women in Canada (2009). https://doi.org/10.3138/9781442689848-006.

Viruell-Fuentes, Edna A., Patricia Y. Miranda, and Sawsan Abdulrahim. "More than Culture: Structural Racism, Intersectionality Theory, and Immigrant Health." Social Science & Medicine 75, no. 12 (2012): 2099–2106. https://doi.org/10.1016/j.socscimed.2011.12.037.

Washington, Patrice C. Real Money Answers for Every Woman: How to Win the Money Game With or Without a Man. New York, NY: Amistad, an Imprint of HarperCollins Publishers, 2016.

Watkins, Michael D. "Picking the Right Transition Strategy." Harvard Business Review (September 7, 2017). https://hbr.org/2009/01/picking-the-right-transition-strategy.

Wingfield, Adia Harvey. "About Those 79 Cents." The Atlantic. Atlantic Media Company (October 21, 2016). https://www.theatlantic.com/business/archive/2016/10/79-cents/504386/.

"Women's Mental Health: Facts, Symptoms & Resources." Regis College Online (May 13, 2020). https://online.regiscollege.edu/blog/womens-mental-health/.

Wu, Tony. "Bicultural Identity." Encyclopedia of Child Behavior and Development (2011), 238–39. https://doi.org/10.1007/978-0-387-79061-9_331.

Yakoboski, Paul J, Annamaria Lusardi, and Andrea Hasler. "The TIAA Institute-GFLEC Personal Finance Index (P-Fin Index)." Global Financial Literacy Excellence Center (GFLEC) (November 22, 2020). https://gflec.org/initiatives/personal-finance-index/.

AUTHOR BIO

Ify A. Ngwudike loves to learn and she finds every experience a great teacher. She has been called a CEO (Chief Encouragement Officer) by friends because she always tries to see the positive in any situation. Her best friend in graduate school once told her she was the worst person to have a fight with because Ify can't help telling her "enemy" what good came out of their "fight". Ify loves to inspire hope in women because she believes in everyday successes and the power of the new, daily chances we get. Though there are struggles in life, joy comes in the morning (metaphorically) and she encourages women in her writing to be grateful, confident and enlightened, recognizing they are gifts to humanity.

Ify currently resides in Canada with her husband and four children. She's lived in three different countries so far and is looking forward to visiting many more as long as she doesn't have to travel with the children. She currently works with adult learners on their personal and academic success and writes about empowerment, personal development, and financial literacy.

www.jaccen.com